The Holy Trinity

THE HOLY TRINITY

Word Water and Blood
Spirit Soul and Person
Father Son and Holy Spirit

THE FATHER GOD ALMIGHTY, GOD AND GOD THE FATHER

HRM King Solomon David Jesse ETE
(King Solomon Spiritual Library)

The Holy Trinity

The Holy Trinity

KING SOLOMON SPIRITUAL LIBRARY
THE GOD ENCYCLOPAEDIA WORD OF INFINITY

BY
THE SPIRIT OF THE FATHER GOD
THROUGH HIS SERVANT
HRM KING SOLOMON DAVID JESSE ETE
(King Solomon Spiritual Library)
Eteroyal Universal Family - BCS

All rights reserved
Copyright © Solomon ETE, 2008
Solomon ETE is hereby identified as author of this work in accordance with Section 77 of the Copyright, Designs and Patents Act 1988

The book cover picture is copyright to Solomon ETE

This book is published by
King Solomon Spiritual Library
P O BOX 27394
London E12 6WW UK
www.kingsolomonspirituallibrary.com
www.ksslibrary.com
ksslibrary@yahoo.co.k
This book is sold subject to the conditions that it shall not, by way of trade or otherwise, be lent, resold, hired out or otherwise circulated without the author's or publisher's prior consent in any form of binding or cover other than that in which it is published and without a similar condition including this condition being imposed on the subsequent purchaser.

A CIP record for this book is available from the British Library
ISBN 978-0-9561498-3-1

Contents

INTRODUCTION   ***9-65***

A: The Word Trinity

B: This Lecture Revelation

C: The Blessed Day

D: Open Your Mind

E: Only The Positive Children Of **THE FATHER GOD**

F: **I AM THE HOLY TRINITY**

G: The Holy Trinity Is Not Three Gods

Part One   ***65-94***
THE HOLY TRINITY – THE FATHER GOD THE HOLY SPIRIT

A: The Spirit

B: Heaven! Unknown place

C: Unhearable

D: Unseenable

E: Untouchable

F: Silent Thought

G: Existence

Part Two   95-137
THE MOTHER GOD THE SOUL

A: The Soul Formation

B: Spiritual World Of Soul Object

C: My Projected Self

D: The Energy Of My Divine Ideas

E: The Supreme Mind Of Creation

F: The Internal Self Creations

G: The Seven Super Souls

Part Three   138-174
THE SON OF GOD THE UNIVERSAL SUPREME WORD

A: The Spirit voice! The Sound Of Creation

B: **Let! I** Say. The First Pronouncement **I** made is, **Let! (YAK)**

C: Physical Creations

D: Manifestation Of My First Physical Home

E: The World Of The Spoken Word

F: Who Owns The World And Creations

G: I THE FATHER GOD I AM THE WORD

Part Four   *174-194*
CONCLUSION

A: The Holy Spirit Of Truth Is The Trinity

B: **I THE FATHER GOD I AM** The Physical Human Being

C: **I THE FATHER GOD I AM The Supreme Word** that lives in every living creature and every living Organism.

D: **I THE FATHER GOD I AM** The Physical Human Being

E: **I THE FATHER GOD I AM THE SUPREME WORD** That Lives In Every Living Creature And Every Living Organism

F: **I THE FATHER GOD** Is All And All And In All Things Brotherhood

G: **I AM THE HOLY TRINITY** The Sum Total Of All Qualities of Manners Of Life

Chapter Two   *195-250*
THE FATHER GOD, GOD AND GOD THE FATHER

Chapter Three   *251-284*
The Inspirational Writers

Chapter One

THE HOLY TRINITY

The Holy Trinity

FATHER'S TALK (GOD PRESENT)

<small>Melchizedek, Fourteenth Simon Canaanite **FATHER** Two Thousand and Nine (AD.OB.BOOI) (Wednesday, Fourteenth February Year Two Thousand and Nine (14.02.2009))</small>

In the Name of Our Lord Jesus Christ, In the Blood of Our Lord Jesus Christ, Now and forever more

THE HOLY TRINITY

Today! It has pleased **ME THE FATHER GOD THE CREATOR OF THE UNIVERSE, THE SUPREME WORD OF EVERLASTING** to give this Lecture Revelation titled **THE HOLY TRINITY** in **Honour** of **THE HOLY TRINITY CELEBRATION on earth on this day,** the Fourteenth of February.

Part One
THE FATHER GOD THE HOLY TRINITY

INTRODUCTION

As **I** always say, **THE FATHER'S TALK (GOD PRESENT) Information** is the WORD **I** permitted to come out from The KING SOLOMON SPIRITUAL LIBRARY to mankind. And it is NOT an ORDINARY PREACHING. It is NOT the WORD via ANGEL. It is the WORD of **THE FATHER GOD PRESENT. THE FATHER'S TALK (GOD PRESENT)** information manifests in the present to reveal **MY PRESENCE** now on earth. It is the **After Those Days Said The Lord Most High.**

THE FATHER'S TALK (GOD PRESENT) is THE TESTIMONY OF THE HOLY SPIRIT ON EARTH. It is the TESTIMONY FOR THE WITNESS OF **THE FATHER'S GOSPEL, THE EVERLASTING GOSPEL** on earth.

There is no need for any soul to be confused or to be misled by any means again. **I** keep this record that will stay for generations upon generations. Since the WORD is living in the physical world, **I** live through the WORD physically for eternity and, because of that this WORD will live for eternity.

The SPIRIT does not die and the WORD can never die. So, this WORD will stay for eternity. And because of that **I** give these Lecture Revelations from time to time. Some of the important information is repeated. It can be repeated seventy-two million times, it does not matter because every **FATHER'S TALK (GOD PRESENT)** Lecture Revelation is One Talk. All spirits are just ONE SPIRIT but manifest as many spirits-souls. Therefore, it does not matter how many **FATHER'S TALK (GOD PRESENT)** Lecture Revelations there are but the components are **One** WORD. For this reason, **I** have given the ability to understand and believe the WORD of the **FATHER'S TALK**

(GOD PRESENT) through **THE SUPREME LOVE**
  THE SUPREME PEACE
  THE SUPREME JOY
  THE SUPREME BLESSING
  THE SUPREME MERCY
  THE SUPREME KINDNESS
  THE SUPREME ONENESS
  THE SUPREME RIGHTEOUSNESS

I put together **THE SUPREME VIRTUES OF THE FATHER GOD** as COMBINED EFFORTS to yield the potency that will maintain this **FATHER'S TALK (GOD PRESENT) INFORMATION** for eternity.

In today's **FATHER'S TALK (GOD PRESENT) I AM** going to reveal and expatiate on **THE HOLY TRINITY** since humankind are confused about **THE HOLY TRINITY.** And also of The Kingdom of God that has manifested on earth for mankind. **I** want everyone to understand these things so that if anyone perishes his or her blood will be upon him or her. It would not be because you did not have access to **The Information.** So, today's information is to help all humankind now and generations upon generations to come to know the right ways, the right behaviours and what is actually positive and belongs to **THE FATHER GOD.** This is so that when you worship evil or Satan or negativism, you know the differences between **THE SUPREME FATHER GOD, THE HOLY SPIRIT OF TRUTH** and things which are not correct.

THE HOLY TRINITY is the GREATEST thing about the history of **THE FATHER GOD.** In fact today's Lecture Revelation is called **SUMMARISING.**

Everything that will be in **THE FATHER'S TALK (GOD PRESENT)** Information, everything that **I** will talk about from now and even forever and what **I** have been talking from the beginning are all inside this **FATHER'S TALK (GOD PRESENT)** Lecture Revelation of today.

This Lecture Revelation is THE SUPREME of all.

This Lecture Revelation is the MAINTENANCE and the INTRODUCTION and also the GUIDANCE as the guiding point, The GUIDE as a MANUAL for all **THE FATHER'S TALK (GOD PRESENT)** Lecture Revelation. This is so for you to know that **THE FATHER'S TALK (GOD PRESENT) Information** itself needs manuals because it needs you to understand what **THE FATHER'S TALK (GOD PRESENT)** means. It needs you to understand the Word of God, starting from the words of prophets of old, which were also **THE FATHER'S TALK.** Even the WORD that **I** preached by **MY** mouth via Jesus Christ and the words of all the prophets are all summarized in this **FATHER'S TALK (GOD PRESENT)** Lecture Revelation. This is so that you will know in order not to be misled.

The Holy Trinity

A: THE WORD TRINITY

What is the meaning of the word **TRINITY?** *TRI-IDEM.*

If you read the following Lecture Revelations:– ***ABASI MU-UDIM THE BLESSED MOTHER, ESIEN EMANA AKPAN, HE IS THE FATHER*** and many other **FATHER'S TALK (GOD PRESENT)** Lecture Revelations you would see that **I** have mentioned this word in them. Nonetheless, today is specifically for this WORD, **TRINITY.** Therefore, what is **TRINITY?**

TRINITY means *Tri idem.*
TRINITY means the **Projection Self.**
TRINITY means **Plural Self.**
TRINITY means **Add On Self, Addition Self.**
TRINITY means that ONE thing can be divided into THREE. And what is the meaning of all that manipulation of the WORD? It means **Love.**

THE HOLY TRINITY actually means **LOVE** because this love manifested the mind of **THE FATHER GOD.**

THE HOLY TRINITY existed when nothing else existed but **THE FATHER GOD.** The manner and the idea of **THE HOLY TRINITY** is to reveal **MYSELF** physically completely on earth so that every human being on earth or any spirit-soul that manifests here on earth should know that the first call is for such a human being or manifested spirit-soul to acknowledge **THE HOLY TRINITY.** If you don't acknowledge **THE HOLY TRINITY** in your system internally and externally, which is the existence of **THE FATHER GOD** being **THE HOLY TRINITY** then you will be doing things wrongly. The result is that you will be misled.

Since **I** do not want anybody to be misled or anyone to mislead another inn the name of being a prophet, a preacher or angel or spirit-soul, it has pleased **ME THE FATHER GOD** this time around to give this Lecture

Revelation to reveal **MYSELF. I AM** revealing **MYSELF** in the capacity that everyone even a layman would understand. Every nature as lower or higher or middle should understand **THE HOLY TRINITY.**

THE HOLY TRINITY will also reveal you as God. **THE HOLY TRINITY** will also reveal everything as one, singular – love; plural – love; subtraction – love; addition – love; multiplication – love; left – love; right – love; up – love; down – love; and no matter wherever you turn to, it is the same one circle of **LOVE!**. That is the actual meaning of **THE FATHER GOD and that is Equality, OOO.** A lot of people argue about the initials **OOO.** Of course, they do not understand that **OOO** means **THE TRINITY GOD.**

Whenever you see that **THE TRINITY GOD** manifest physically is celebrated and recognised, then know that everything is well finally, finally and finally. This is because we have come

The Holy Trinity

to the central point. **I** have now come to the **CONCLUSION** part of all the **REVELATIONS** about **THE FATHER GOD, THE SPIRIT, THE SOUL, THE PHYSICAL** and so on. They are all centralized in **THE TRINITY GOD.** So, **THE HOLY TRINITY** CELEBRATION DAY is to mark out that everything in Heaven and on Earth centralized has come together and manifested in **THE TRINITY GOD.**

THE TRINITY GOD must be something that deals with the WHOLE and can be touched. You can hear, you can see and you can touch. **THE TRINITY GOD** is not something that is only in spirit. It is not something you can only hear and cannot see. It is not something that you can see but cannot touch. You must hear, you must see and you must touch. That is the meaning of **THE HOLY TRINITY GOD.**

THE HOLY TRINITY GOD is something that you cannot deny! If you deny **THE HOY TRINITY GOD** then, you are a damned person and a damned soul! **THE HOLY TRINITY GOD** is that last opportunity open for people to believe, because when you believe in **THE HOLY TRINITY GOD** you have no problems again. Anybody who would not believe in **THE HOLY TRINITY GOD** is a wanted person, because you believe SPIRIT and you believe SOUL but you would not believe the physical manifestation. Since you don't believe the physical manifestation of **THE FATHER GOD,** then you do not believe **THE HOLY TRINITY GOD** and that means you are damned!

Without any soul believing in **THE HOLY TRINITY GOD** the person's soul cannot be saved. Therefore, **I** brought this Lecture Revelation of today to the entire mankind, whether you are baptised in the water or not. **I** now baptize you with the Holy Spirit through this word of truth if you believe in the name and blood of Our Lord Jesus Christ now and forever more Amen. If you believe this

The Holy Trinity

Lecture Revelation information as the word of life then you are saved. Also, if you believe this Lecture Revelation and accept that you are a part of **ME THE HOLY TRINITY** then you are saved. **THE HOLY TRINITY GOD** is the final centralized point of **ME THE FATHER GOD**. That is why **I** said that the Word **TRINITY** is the TOTAL of everything.

THE HOLY SPIRIT IS THE TRINITY as one thing that has projected to be three, but it is one in essence. Why would one thing project to be three? That is what you are going to hear now.

When that **THING** was a thing and not hearable, not seen and not touchable, it could NOT be called **TRINITY.** And that means that it was in the dark. No light. No idea. Who knows who know, nobody knows. So, if who does not know who knows and nobody knows then it means there is no God in the physical reality. But if you know and you know what you now know, then you know that **THE FATHER GOD** has manifested physically as **THE HOLY TRINITY GOD.** That is what **THE HOLY TRINITY** Lecture Revelation of today is about.

B: **THIS LECTURE REVELATION**

This Lecture Revelation is what you must understand as **THE FATHER'S TALK (GOD PRESENT).** It is not a vision and it is not a prophecy. Nonetheless, vision and prophecy are contained inside. This is **GOD'S** WORD – **THE FATHER GOD'S** WORD. **I, THE FATHER GOD** talks direct and keep the records.

This WORD will not fade away for generations upon generations. It is not an old WORD and it is not a new WORD. It is not the last WORD. And it is not the first WORD. It is the WORD that is round, round and round. It is in a circle. You can use **THE FATHER'S TALK (GOD PRESENT)** information in the morning, in the

The Holy Trinity

afternoon, in the evening. You can use **THE FATHER'S TALK (GOD PRESENT)** Lecture Revelations in Heaven and you can use them on earth and you can use them in the Paradise of Souls. You can die and go now, but you will come back to use **THE FATHER'S TALK (GOD PRESENT)** Information. You will be given birth to on earth to meet **THE FATHER'S TALK (GOD PRESENT)** and you grow up to use **THE FATHER'S TALK (GOD PRESENT)** Lectures Revelations. **THE FATHER'S TALK (GOD PRESENT)** is round in figure. That is why the information always starts with **THE FATHER'S TALK (GOD PRESENT).**

Whenever you come across The Word of GOD, The Living Word of GOD, it is **THE PRESENT** OF **THE FATHER GOD** because **I AM** living in the WORD. **THE SPIRIT** lives in **THE WORD** and **THE WORD** lives in man. And that is, human beings. And that is these Lecture Revelations as **THE FATHER'S TALK (GOD PRESENT).**

C: **THE BLESSED DAY**

Today is a **Blessed Day** for all humankind. **I** use this **FATHER'S TALK (GOD PRESENT)** Lecture Revelation to bless the entire universe, the entire humankind, all positive children of **THE FATHER GOD,** those who celebrate the **TRINITY DAY, THE TRINITY WEEK,** the actual **TRINITY DAY I have** marked out for eternity on the **Fourteenth of the Eleventh month of the year (February)**. There is a spiritual name for this period but in your own month you call it February. **I** have given a complete Lecture Revelation about that.

This day as **I** revealed before is a **Blessed Day. I AM** going to reveal the importance of this day. First of all, **I** want reveal that the first thing that happened on the **Fourteenth of the Eleventh month of the year (February)** when **I, THE FATHER GOD** came to the Garden of Eden after **I** creating Adam and recreated him by removing one of his ribs to create Eve. The day **I** actually carried out that operation was the **Fourteenth day of the Eleventh month of the year.** That was the day **I** took Adam to **MY OBOT UTIM** (Spiritual Hospital) and took one of his ribs to create Eve. But in the SPIRIT of **MY** SPIRIT, in the Internal Memory of **MYSELF** with all Heavenly Hosts of which you will hear of some in this Lecture Revelation, it was the same day in the spirit soul that Lucifer denied and refused to worship **The Son of God, THE UNIVERSAL SUPREME WORD.** It was the same day of **Fourteenth of (February) the Eleventh month of the year** that **I** named her the **oxymoron** spirit-soul.

When the time came back to that same **Fourteenth February which is called 'ADDIAN DAY' in spirit meaning Meeting Time**, **I** decided to extract the part of **oxymoron** spirit self away from Adam to create

The Holy Trinity

another person that is the **Fe** part. When you read the Lecture Revelation titled **ABASI MU-UDIM (THE BLESSED MOTHER)** you will know more about the **Fe** part and other vital information contained therein.

So, **I** created the **Fe** part and named that one Eve, the extraction self of Adam. They became separate selves but linked up to one SPIRIT SELF. The idea of doing that was so that **I** could then use Adam as **MY** Positive Self and Eve as **MY** Positive Self to manifest **MY** Glory.

After **I** have successfully done that, **I** instructed Adam and Eve saying that 'now you are two separate human beings but are connected to one entity of THE WHOLE **HE IS THE SPIRIT.** *However, since that* **oxymoron** *spirit-soul was still there, as The Negative Spoken Word as part of the Silent Thought of Creation, it was not yet divine to differentiate. So I banned them from eating from the tree that **I** put in the Middle of Garden*

The Holy Trinity

of Eden. **I** said that they should not eat because if they ate the fruit, what **I** had extracted from them would go back into them.

Lucifer being the Negative Thought, the **oxymoron** heard the instruction **I** that gave to Adam and Eve. She then planned to bypass that order, because the negative self always wants to spoil what the positive self arranges. In order to achieve her evil ambition Lucifer came on exactly the **Fourteenth of February** to the Garden of Eden and used serpent for that purpose.

Serpent was male as the first energy of an animal nature and he was very, very tricky and powerful. **I** created serpent for *cut-join*. What **I** mean by *cut-join* is the corner spirit-soul, a corner trigger nature, but it was positive at that stage. *Cut-join* is something used to repair things that have slight problems. If you have something that needs repair, you would retouch and retouch until you repair the thing that has problem. You cut, join and paste on the problematic part to repair it. It is called **cornarisance.**

Cornarisance is like using a marker, paint and a brush that is used on something to clean away and cover up an error or an eraser to erase away something. **I** gave **cornarisance** to serpent because **I** made serpent the senior animal of all the instincts of animal nature.

Serpent was the head of all the three living creatures, which are **animals, birds** and **fishes,** to oversee all the behaviours of other animals because they were and still are primitive creations. They don't know anything. So, because of that small instinct **I** elevated the serpent with, Lucifer thought the serpent being a male part of animal nature, she would be able to control Adam and Eve through the serpent. Why did **I** create serpent in that nature?

The Holy Trinity

The creation of the serpent was from the rush of the water ***mmong ikpor, (UKWOH)***. What **I** call ***mmong ikpor*** is the rush of the water. **I, THE FATHER GOD** projected **MYSELF** as the **Water** and generated **MYSELF** on top of the **Water** as **The Supreme Air of Nature**. During this time, the air became very powerful from the rushing water. The ***ikpor mmong,*** that is, ***udim ikpor mmong,*** which is the rushing force of water through the air, formulated the fast current. When **I** saw that ***udim ikpor mmong*** that is, the **Rushing Force Of The Water** through the air that formulated the fast current was over flowing, **I** decided to put up a barrier to curb the overflowing of current. That fast current was what **I** took to create the nature of this animal energy and gave it the current power called '**URUK IBIOK'** or **URUK IDIOK** (bay) serpent.

    I took this serpent to cross over the sea so that when **MY** rushing current wants to over flow, it would barrier it. The water would go and anchor there. The water would go *wooooaaaaahhh*! And stop there. It served as a bay, like a natural harbour. That is called **Pavement of the Sea, River or Water.**

The **serpent** represents that current power energy of the nature across the sky, water and land. That is, in the physical earth it is **serpent,** but it is called **dragon,** which is the **Dragging Force of the Waters** that includes the oceans, seas, rivers and so on. So, the energy of the **dragging force of The Sea** is what **I** took to create **dragon,** but in the physical energy it is the animal called **serpent**. They are the same thing. The actual force of that energy called **dragon** lives in the water. It is ***uruk ikpor mmong.*** So the actual snake or serpent as you have now is formed by water energy. **I** will go further into this later.

The Holy Trinity

I gave a Lecture Revelation about dragon and that dragon was a soul object that can fly. It was not negative until it joined the **Oxymoron,** because **I** used carnal energy as water to create it. Being that **I** used the carnal energy to create dragon, it was not all that positive. Well, since **I AM** not going into that in full **I AM** only telling you that Lucifer was able to infuse her energy into serpent and used serpent to deceive Adam and Eve because of the carnal nature of serpent. The day Lucifer successfully did this was the same **Fourteenth February.** All these things happened after **I** have finished all creations and when **I** finally created man in the end.

Let **ME** reveal one of the mysteries about **Fourteenth February.**

Fourteenth February represents the **Seven Spirits of Objects Soul Creation** plus **Seven Spirits soul of the Creation of the days of the week and another Seven Spirit**

The Holy Trinity

souls of Human Nature. There all Seven Spirits of Creation is one. It stands for **God Of The Earth and** that is, the Seven Days of the Week that **I** started and finished creations. Had it been that **I** did not keep one Spirit safe so as to be three in capacity, then Lucifer would have succeeded in her plans and as **I AM** talking now it would have been a different story. Nonetheless, **I** know things before things happen.

    I AM ALL KNOWING. **I** outsmart the First because **I AM** before The First and **I AM** also The First- you know, you know. **I** knew that such a thing as **Lucifer's** betrayal would happen because **I** make things to happen in advance so that **I** would do corrections as **MY Second Thought.** And when **I** brought **MY Second Thought, Lucifer's** impression was then that it was her doing. **Lucifer** did not know that **I** was the one that did that. Whilst in **The First Thought,** the elementary self thinks that, **it** was the one that has made the mistake; **it** does not know that **I AM** the **ONE** that has had the **Second Thought** in advance. **I** use the First thought for experiment and **I** make corrections with the second thought.

This Lecture Revelation **I AM** giving today is called **Technical Soul Information.** So, whomever that transcribes and proofreads this should use Technical Spiritual Understanding to do the job well, otherwise that will not be.

Continuing with what **I** was saying, **I AM** merely making this point in this Lecture Revelation to reveal that, there was purpose for **ME** resting on one day as it is said that God rested on the seventh day. That one day was the energy to protect **MYSELF** against such incidents of adulterousness of the infidel **Oxymoron** and her group of selves. If **I** did not do that, then Lucifer would have come to deceive Adam and Eve on the Twenty-first day and that would have been the end of

The Holy Trinity

the year. Everything that needed done would have finished then. **I** would not have had any time again to make corrections before **EKARA USEN** (the Continue Turning Round day). Let **ME** explain to you why that would have been.

    Fourteenth was the **Physical Seven** and the **Soul Seven** but the **Spiritual Seven** still remained for **ME,** which **I AM** now using to make new creations and make everything new. The total of **Twenty-One Days** is for a **Period Of Life** because these twenty-one days makes a **Cycle Of Life.** Since one Cycle Of Life and another Cycle Of Life plus another Cycle Of Creation equals twenty-one days through seven multiplied by three equals twenty one, it means, one Cycle was not used. **I** preserved it. Lucifer did not know that. Her knowledge did not reach this area. As such she quickly came on the **Fourteenth** (the next Cycle after the first) to challenge **ME** by deceiving Adam and Eve through introducing the act of fornication to them. And that is why on that **Fourteenth February** Lucifer went and deceived Adam and Eve by introducing the act of fornication to them and they ate the forbidden fruit and spoke the first negative words.

The first negative words that the serpent thought Adam and Eve to speak were "*I AM NAKED*." This is the first time in the history of mankind that **I** have revealed this. "*I AM NAKED*" were the first nonsense words, the first negative words ever that the human being spoke. ***"I AM NAKED" MEANS "I AM DEAD!"*** Naked means Death! When someone is naked it means death. It is only **THE SPIRIT** that can be naked, but if any physical thing becomes naked that thing is dead. Therefore, **I** did not expect such words from a human being **I** created and covered with life (LOVE). For such human being to say "*I AM NAKED*." it means that you are dead. On what day did Adam speak that word? It was today the **Fourteenth February, the Eleventh month of the year**.

On the **Fourteenth of February,** Lucifer went in spirit soul to the serpent and asked the serpent if 'he' could help her to convince Eve to have fornication with Adam. Don't forget that if Lucifer were a male spiritual self, she would have gone straight and suppressed Eve and had union with her to give birth to Lucifer herself or himself as the case would have been, physically on earth, just as **I** created Adam physically on earth.

Let **ME THE FATHER GOD** explain this again. **Lucifer** is a **Female Self** and she has no male organ to produce seed. She therefore, borrowed a seed from serpent that was the male part on the land. Serpent was the suitable candidate to do that job for Lucifer, who is now called Satan. That is why Satan is mistake. Satan is error. *That First Negative Word That Adam*

Spoke Was "Naked", the First Mistake Is What Is Called Satan, as Wicked, Error, and Wrong.

How did you know you were naked? Why and how did you come to know that? **I** ask because that was the first time that Adam and Eve knew that something was bad. That first word **"NAKED"** means something is bad. **"I AM NAKED!"** Means 'I have committed sin.' How did you know that it is sin that you have committed, if your eyes were not opened? So, instead of their eyes to open to know **THE FATHER GOD** and to know about love and to know about equality, and to know about peace, and to know about oneness and all the good things, their eyes opened for **"NAKED" "WICKED" "NEGATIVE."** And from that time death got established in the Garden of Eden. That was why the first energy of "**WICKED**" manifested through Cain, who represents animals, the serpent as Satan.

The Holy Trinity

Now **I** will not go too far into this on this **Blessed Day** that is, why **I** made this day the **Fourteenth February, the Eleventh month of the year** to be **The Blessed Day.** In a nutshell, **I** made today to be **THE HOLY TRINITY DAY** to superimpose on all the negative occurrences and particularly the negative celebration they call Valentine Celebration. Nonetheless, don't forget that this **Fourteenth February** as the **Eleventh month of the year** is the day **I** made plural blessings by creating the womb to manifest many human beings. It was the actual day to manifest **God Of Multitudes** which is Eve **I** created.

Lucifer knew that with this creation, **THE FATHER GOD** would have multitudes and lots of glories and lots of good things would be established. And that is why she quickly went to infuse that evil thought, that error back into the system to pollute the system. And in truth the system became polluted.

The Holy Trinity

The reason **I** called **MYSELF** in ALL TOTALITIES, including EVERY SELF that 'Let Us Create Man In Our Own Image And Likeness' was that, after the creation of all things there was no human being on earth. And **I** was busy controlling everything including **Lucifer** who was very **beautiful** and was the **Sweet Voiced Self.** She was an entertainer with beauty, glorious and all things beautiful! And her energy was manipulated in the water beneath.

People do not know the meaning of Heaven. As people do not know the meaning of Heaven, they think Heaven is up and Hell is down. It is not like that. The Water Planet, not the sea or ocean you see but in a place well underneath the ocean, there is another city. It is a planet beneath the sea where the spirit-soul mermaids live, which is the actual Water Planet. **I** revealed this in the Lecture Revelation titled ***THE SPIRITUAL NATURE OF A***

"WHITEMAN" LIGHT SKIN HUMANS.

The Nature of The Mother, Lucifer, which **I** created to be beautiful was sweet voiced and glorious in apparel, and was from the Water Planet. And the humans from that planet are called **Basement In Creation.**

Basement In Creation Natures are those natures that grow underneath the sea as the Mermaid Queendom. Most of the negative, carnal and evil ideas that are practiced are all from there. Even the Seven Angels that **I** refused to return to the **Upper Self** of **THE FATHER GOD** were captured by Lucifer that is also as Satan as he, and said 'come and work for me, I don't mind.' So they are all working for him. However, that Mermaid Queendom was not a negative place. **I** created the Mermaid Queendom for proper beauty and sweet voices and to make beautiful things happen to maintain the physical world. All the flashing things of life and all beautiful things are from the **Basement In Creation** world. Anyway, that is not what **I AM** going into again now. **I** just slot it in so that you will have a proper understanding about this Lecture Revelation.

Because negativism captured and ruled that place, the negative spirit-soul and his agents use those beautiful and carnal things to flatter and deceive mankind on earth today. But now! **I HAVE CAPTURED THAT PLANET COMPLETELY!** And **I** have turned everything to be **FATHER GOD! FATHER GOD! FATHER GOD!** -Because from the beginning of time everything came from **ME THE FATHER GOD.** Without **I, THE FATHER GOD** nothing exists.

Lucifer introduced the act of fornication that is, adultery as adulteration of the energy template of **THE DIVINE GOD.** That act of fornication was the adulteration of the template of **THE FATHER GOD'S** energy. And that is what **I** call Adultery. To introduce a foreign

The Holy Trinity

substance into an original substance and spoil that original thing is adulteration. It is an act of wickedness that inflicts pure pain on the owner of the original substance. And that was what happened between Lucifer and **I, THE FATHER GOD.**

So, on the **Fourteenth February, the Eleventh month of the year,** the cycle came back to the same day that **I** created Adam and Eve just as the cycle of your current year.

What Lucifer did was that she worked through the cycle. In the spirit, **I** do not have 'Time' because **I AM THE TIME**, and **I** do not have months and years. What **I** have is **O** that is, **round, circle.**

OUR Cycle of Time is symbolic of the **cycle** period of the monthly menstrual flow of NATURE of the WOMB (women menstrual period). It is called **Cycle Of Creation** or **Cycle of Nature. OUR** time works in the round nature of the circle. **OUR** day comes back to meet the day. **OUR**

The Holy Trinity

night comes back to meet the night. That is how Nature works, in a cycle. The Spiritual Moon or the Natural Moon, the Natural Day, the Natural Time, Natural Year, and Natural Generation, all work in a cycle. They each move and come back to meet the point that they left. That is the cycle. Therefore, the cycle of time rotates and comes back to meet the same cycle of the **Fourteenth February, the Eleventh month of the year.** And that meant that something was to happen on that day.

On that **Fourteenth February, the Eleventh month of the year, I** first finished the creations but **I** left one **spirit object** unused. When the same cycle came round to that same, day and **I** corrected the creation of Adam and Eve in one body. **I** made Eve to be separate from Adam and the **I** gave her a **Womb Of Nature.** Then on that, same cycle of the **Fourteenth February, the Eleventh month of the year** Lucifer came back and deceived Adam and Eve. In that same cycle, when **I** came back to see **MY** farm and to see what was happening there, Adam and Eve told **ME THE FATHER GOD** that they were **"*NAKED*"** on the same day on that cycle day of **Fourteenth February, the of Eleventh month of the year.** That was the day they spoke the **first evil word.** That same cycle was the same day that Cain was born. **Cain** was born on the **Fourteenth of February, the Eleventh month of the year** to mark out the evil day that serpent or Lucifer or Satan deceived Adam and Eve and spoilt **MY Divine Product** and drove **ME THE FATHER GOD** away from **MY** home.

Okay! As Cain was born, he then grew. And every fourteenth day **I** remember that day and Lucifer also remembers that day but **I** wanted to earmark that day for positive remembrances because where you put your feet as positive, Satan or the negative one will also try to put his

The Holy Trinity

feet there but you must counteract it so that you conquer.

On the **Fourteenth February, the Eleventh month of the year, I** ordered the two sons of Adam to identify themselves by showing appreciation to **ME THE FATHER GOD.** They each had to use the product of their work for an offering and that was purely for identification purpose. Abel used very good gift to show appreciation on that day, the **Fourteenth February** to **ME THE FATHER GOD.** And **I** accepted it, while Cain on his part, brought very bad gifts that were not good for anything and presented them to **ME THE FATHER GOD.** And **I** did not accept those horrible gifts from him. Cain did not yield from **MY Positive Spirit Self** therefore why should **I** accept that dreadful gift from him? So, that day was a **Blessed Day for Abel.** And it was a remarkable day, a day immortalized forever as a day of

The Holy Trinity

identity for all the **Positive Children of THE FATHER GOD.**

When the cycle came back to reach the day of the **fourteenth February, the Eleventh month of the year** again, Cain killed Abel. It was outside the gate of the Garden of Eden where **I** drove Adam and Eve. And the place where Cain killed Abel was named '**IYIP**' (Egypt), where the first blood was spilled.

When **THE WORD** came back as the Father of Abel, **I** sent Him to (IYIP) Egypt. Do you know why **I** sent the young Jesus to Egypt? It was because Abel was killed there. That place called Egypt is blood in meaning. Egypt means blood. That actual place called Egypt means blood as the Blood Land. That was where the shedding of the blood of Abel took place. The spirit-soul **Oxymoron**, the actual vampire's home thought he did very well to kill Abel. He killed Abel so that Abel would not have any tribe. All these problems are fights against the plurality of the positive children of **THE FATHER GOD** on earth. **I AM** telling you the cause of events and the secrets of all these wars. The secrets and the reason for fighting of all these wars are to eliminate the actual positive offspring as the tribe of **GOD** so that negativism would cover the whole earth. That is the actual thing going on in the world.

Do not forget that when animals, birds and fishes were plenty and occupied everywhere, there were no human beings at all. All the living creatures then including animals, birds and fishes were fighting and killing themselves, just as they are doing till today. Nothing good was coming from them. No wisdom. No good idea and mostly no speaking of words. Everywhere and everything was just *mmooooohhh! Mmooooohhh!* Darkness! No light! So, **I** continued exhausting **MY energy** fuelling the earth for nothing! What can animals do? They go about eating grass and eating themselves also. Big fish swallow small fish; big animal eat small animal. What was the improvement of the land that is, the earth? But everyday the sun would shine bright in the sky. Everyday rain would fall to water the earth. **I** continued to maintain the land for nothing with no improvement whatsoever from these creatures.

For **ME** therefore, to improve the earth **I** SAID, LET **US** CREATE MAN IN **OUR** OWN **IMAGE** AND **LIKENESS**. **OUR** own image and likeness is so that the world, the whole earth would be fruitful. And the Light of the World, the physical WORD should live on earth and become the overseer of all that **HE** has created.

Where would this **WORD** live? **HE** would live in a particular house that **I** would create and that is the House **I** call man! Adam! Human being! And **I** put **MYSELF** there to oversee all **MY** creations.

The Holy Trinity

When animals saw human, they were okay at the early stage. And marvelled thus, 'who is this one that has come and He is very handsome and the other very beautiful. They are knowledgeable and can even speak too'. They all were subject to Adam and He gave them names and directed them. Adam started to tell them what to do. He controlled them, gave them duties and implemented division of labour. He told them that they should not fight and that they should love one another. They obeyed Adam and did everything for Adam and Eve but all that stopped when Adam and Eve derailed. When Adam spoke to the animals after he and Eve disobeyed **ME** they did not like it and would not obey. They stopped going on errands. But in the earlier time everything was fine but for one animal that did not like Adam and Eve.

The only animal that was jealous of Adam and Eve was the serpent that

The Holy Trinity

believed he was the king of the land. That is why **I** say that if you are jealous put yourself in prayers because Satan must surely use you. You become a hope for Satan. Had it been serpent was not jealous Satan would not have used serpent for her handiwork. The serpent was not a bad animal. **I** told you **I** created serpent for a good purpose but he had jealousy in him and so became jealous because he saw Adam and Eve handsome and beautiful, talking and describing things, giving them names and controlling, managing and directing them. So, the serpent became really jealous and questioned that who is this one now that every animal listens to? The serpent followed other animals to bow down to Adam but that was only pretence. The serpent was not happy at all at the new arrivals.

Lucifer knew that there was an animal called serpent that **THE FATHER GOD** made a bit clever and gave a little of knowledge so she

The Holy Trinity

decided to use that one because its eyes were opened. He had a bit of an elevated nature. So Lucifer went straight in spirit soul and spoke with a very small spirit voice and told serpent to go and deceive Eve by introducing the act of fornication as, sexual immorality to Eve. He made Eve's body tingle with desire. He made Eve know that she was wasting time by not having that with Adam. He did all these things in the spirit-soul of witchcraft. He was doing it in an elementary spirit soul. It was not done physically but he made Eve to have awareness of herself.

On the first fourteenth day Eve had the first blood issue from her body. That was the first menstruation that Eve ever had because of the interruption of Serpent in the spirit-soul with Eve. When Eve saw blood came out from her body, she said to Adam 'MOKUT UNANG ISONG' 'I have seen a wound without a cut; I have seen something that is 'IYIP',

The Holy Trinity

'***UMIANA***' 'IDEM' blood, what is that?' As a result of this, they carried leaves and covered their bodies. That was the introduction of the act of sexuality between Adam and Eve that made them say they were naked because they started to see themselves naked. This all took place on the **Fourteenth February and all** was intended for **MY** plan to fail but **MY** plans never fail.

When Eve then got pregnant with a child by inspiration of serpent, she gave birth to Cain. Cain was not a child of Adam per se just like Jesus Christ was not a son of Joseph per se. He was a Son of God. So, Cain was a son of Lucifer, the serpent, vampire. He was the first negative human-animal on earth.

Okay! When Abel came on earth as a human-God with the spirit motivated by the positive spirit of **THE FATHER GOD** from Adam so that the offspring of **THE FATHER GOD** as positivism would be

The Holy Trinity

established on earth, the negative spirit-soul was not happy and wanted to devour Abel. He wanted to eat Abel in an evil way but since Abel donated the fattest ram that represented himself for that sacrifice to show appreciation to **ME THE FATHER GOD, I** held his life spiritually. **Cain then Cain killed Abel** on the same **Fourteenth February, the Eleventh month of the year** on the spot called '**IYIP**' (Egypt).

That spot called Egypt is the entrance between the Mermaid Planet and the world of Human Souls on earth. Egypt is the boundary between the Indian Ocean and the tropical areas of Atlantic Ocean where the dragon lives. That was where **I** flung dragon to and it made its home there and lived there. Egypt is also the boundary of Africa. Egypt therefore, is Africa. However, Egypt is where all the negative spirit-souls come out physically to pollute the world and establish what they call carnal

The Holy Trinity

civilization (IDIOK NTATEEYEIN) BAD OPEN EYE. The reason civilization started in Egypt is because that was where **I** put up the barrier and that was where Lucifer introduced the act of fornication to Adam and Eve and because of that they became the first to have civilization of carnal life. As a result of that also, Lucifer established her first throne there called *cotapo.*

Cotapo is god of evil stone. The actual vampire, the actual witchcraft and wizard spirit-soul is called **COTAPO**. That was what the Egyptians worshipped as god during the time of the original Pharaoh. The god of evil called *cotapo* was what they worshipped.

The first negative part of womanhood manifested as *cotapo* and was called Pharaoh, the god of Shemon, the energy mammon of wealth on earth as Sheba. Pharaoh spiritually was not a man. The first nature of Pharaoh was a woman and that was the witchcraft in the self.

And the spiritual soul energy of that Pharaoh was called Sheba therefore that is the god of Sheba and that is why Sheba was wealth. And because of Sheba, Lucifer thought that she had captured all the earth and ruled the earth through wealth. She used that to entice all children of God to follow her and to worship her. And she became very hardened, very, very hardened.

The meaning of *cotapo* is *God of Womanhood*, the Queendom World, the Queendom glory. It is from the Water. I will leave this here for now.

However, before, I end this one here I have to give you this piece of information that *Valentine* is the namesake of *cotapo,* that is also *the god of fornication.* This Valentine Celebration, which is celebration of fornication, was the same thing that Sheba the god of fornication established. It means they use fornication to generate the wealth of the world. **Valentine's Day is to**

The Holy Trinity

celebrate the day that Lucifer introduced the acts of sexuality. That was the same day Queen Sheba used to have her celebration, which she convinced King Solomon to dance with her.

The reason **I** instructed King Solomon to establish **THE HOLY TRINITY DAY CELEBRATION** on the **Fourteenth February, the Eleventh month of the year**, is to superimpose on the evil celebration of this day they called Valentine Day. And also, to pay back the debt He has with **ME** when He went and danced with Queen Sheba in the throne of the god of adulteration on earth.

TODAY **FOURTEENTH FEBRUARY** HRM KING SOLOMON DAVID JESSE ETE HAS ESTABLISHED **THE HOLY TRINITY DAY CELEBRATION.**

And on the same **Fourteenth February, the Eleventh month of the year, I THE HOLY SPIRIT OF TRUTH** SAID THAT IF ANYBODY CAN ANNOY **ME** TO DESTROY THE WORLD

The Holy Trinity

AGAIN, **I** WOULD GIVE SUCH A PERSON A HANDSOME REWARD. BUT IT WILL NOT HAPPEN!

I will not destroy the world like before because all that Lucifer is doing is for **ME** to continue to destroy **MY** works. He is the destroyer. He would come to **ME,** 'Oh God be annoyed and destroy this. Oh look at what the people are doing. Destroy them.' **I** said that **I** made a rainbow to remind **ME** not to destroy the world with water again. When the water wanted to flow over and flood the world to destroy the world, **I** said no. Instead of water **I** will use fire to destroy the negative things in the world so that **I** still retain the ones that are positive.

Now, **I** can only destroy all evil and negative things, burn them with fire, but not by water. **I** will not destroy the world again by water which the nature motherhood. Motherhood nature of water has finished her acting. Now it is **FATHERHOOD NATURE! FATHER GOD! I THE**

The Holy Trinity

FATHER GOD will burn and destroy all negativism! And all positives will remain on earth.

Having said all that, Abel established **THE HOLY TRINITY WEEK and THE TRINITY DAY CELEBRATION** a long, long time ago on the **FOURTEENTH FEBRUARY OF ELEVENTH MONTHS OF THE YEAR**. It was the same day that Abel was born. It was the same day spiritually that Abel was killed. It was the same day that Lucifer convinced Eve to eat the forbidden fruit. Also that same day she Lucifer came back to establish Valentine Day on earth for her carnal energy, so that the whole world would fornicate and call it love. That was the same day that Queen Sheba used to dance to god of "Sexual Immorality" and deceitfully and cunningly called Valentine 'Love Day'. That same day was for *cotapo the god of evil* that the Egyptians worshipped and that was Pharaoh, carved god.

The same **Fourteenth February** was the day **I** revealed that the children of Israel should go and register their names in the land of Bethlehem, the Tribe of David. The same day **I** kept for baptism day at the River Jordan when John first took baptism, but before then it was not called baptism day it was named the identification day. That is, when the child had to be circumcised for identification. Therefore, this day **FOURTEENTH FEBRUARY, the Eleventh month of every year** is the day to separate the sheep from the goat.

IF YOU ARE **POSITIVE** YOU CELEBRATE **THE TRINITY DAY.**

IF YOU ARE **NEGATIVE** YOU CELEBRATE **VALENTINE'S DAY**.

Nonetheless, **I, THE FATHER GOD** have superimposed **THE TRINITY DAY** on Valentine's Day on this day the **Fourteenth February, the Eleventh month of the year** for eternity.

The Holy Trinity

This day, the **Fourteenth February, the Eleventh month of the year** now is the glorious day to celebrate **THE HOLY TRINITY GOD, THE FATHER SON AND HOLY SPIRIT OF TRUTH** represented in human nature, the **Water,** the **Blood** and the **Spirit.** That is why **I** said that the day is a **BLESSED DAY.**

D: **OPEN YOUR MIND**

Open Your Mind so that you can receive the blessing of today; so that you can understand what **I** mean; so that Satan will not be able to tempt you. If you do not open your mind for the Holy Spirit, then you have given yourself for Satan to tempt you. Anyone that cannot control his or her mind will be tempted by Satan. Nevertheless, by giving this **FATHER'S TALK (GOD PRESENT)** Lecture Revelation of today there is no evil again that can overcome the children of **GOD**, in the name and blood of Our Lord Jesus Christ.

All children of **THE FATHER GOD** will be able to control their mind and overcome evil minds. And they will be shining as stars in **THE FATHER'S KINGDOM**. So, always open your mind and then **I, THE HOLY SPIRIT** as **I** have now vowed to live with all mankind for eternity will be in you. **I** will not run away again from mankind. **I** have forgiven humankind through the '**Blood of Our Lord Jesus Christ'**. And that is why you should forgive one another and have love. Then **I** will continue to live with you and change you for **MYSELF.**

E: **ONLY THE POSITIVE CHILDREN OF THE FATHER GOD**

It is **Only the Positive Children of THE FATHER GOD** that will take this WORD that will have access to this blessing, this improvement and this elevation, because **I** have used this Lecture Revelation to elevate your soul, your spirit and you physical nature. And anything you do from now onwards becomes elevated. Therefore, you have become an elevated Object Soul from now upward.

And even if you are an evolutional human-animal, human-bird or human-fish and you believe this Lecture Revelation because this is **FATHER'S TALK GOD PRESENT** then **I** will motivate your spirit-soul and elevate it away from what you are and you will become the spirit-soul that worships **THE FATHER GOD**. And you will have an evolutional energy to the positive side of **ME THE FATHER GOD**.

F: **I AM THE HOLY TRINITY**

I AM THE HOLY TRINITY MYSELF, FATHER SON AND THE HOLY SPIRIT with all the Holy Ghosts. Holy Ghosts are all the positive souls that have finished their assignments and come back to **ME THE FATHER GOD.** Their souls are preserved to become Holy Ghosts.

These are the souls **I** use to preserve and maintain the root and tribe of positivism of **ME THE FATHER GOD.** So they are the sheep not the wolves and not goats. This means that they are the positive children of **THE FATHER GOD,** the positive tribe of **THE FATHER GOD** on earth.

These are those who have no arrogance, those who have no pomposity, who cannot kill, who cannot be wicked in any way and cannot destroy. They are positive. Their duty is to preserve lives and love one another, have mercy, have oneness, equality and kindness. Those are the sheep as the tribe of the children of **GOD.**

G: **THE HOLY TRINITY IS NOT THREE SPIRITS**

I THE FATHER GOD, THE TRINITY GOD, I AM NOT **THREE.** But **I AM** like a voltage that gives current, which is divided into three channels. The faces are Positive face,

Negative face and Neutral. When you put them together, they give you the energy current that produces light. That is why **MY Energy** operates under those capacities, but that does NOT mean **I AM** Three.

The Father, Son and Holy Spirit is ONE entity *HE IS THE SPIRIT.* But before **I** can manifest **MY** glory and bring everything to perfect fruition, **I** project **MYSELF** into three capacities so that all will be well.

I hope you understand this WORD, but if you do not, then fast and pray.

This is the end of **Part One – THE HOLY TRINITY INTRODUCTION.**

After the **INTRODUCTION,** Part Two of this **FATHER'S TALK (GOD PRESENT)** called **THE HOLY TRINITY** is **THE SPIRIT.**

THE HOLY TRINITY

PART TWO
THE FATHER GOD "THE SPIRIT"

A: THE SPIRIT

THE SPIRIT as **I** have already said in many of **THE FATHER'S TALK (GOD PRESENT)** Lecture Revelations is silent in form, blank in form, zero in form therefore, it is the more you look, the less you see – **ZAKROLL.** There is no home of the **SPIRIT** that anybody can say **I** visited the Spiritual Realm or **I** visited Spiritual Home. Or that this is where **SPIRIT** lives. Or **SPIRIT** is here. **THE SPIRIT** is the most secret, most mysterious and the utmost supreme of all things that no human being can fathom. Not even **Gods** understand **THE SPIRIT.**

What you call **GOD** is after **I THE SPIRIT** has projected **MY SPIRIT SELF** out from **THE RAW SPIRIT** and formed **GOD** from **THE FATHER** or **THE FATHER GOD.** The **FATHER**

The Holy Trinity

GOD is **MY** projected **SELF** that formed an **OBJECT SOUL** manipulated by **MY SUPREME THOUGHT ENERGY.** That is **THE FATHER GOD, THE SUPREME THOUGHT.** And from this **FATHER GOD** emerged **THE WORD** called **THE UNIVERSAL SUPREME WORD and** THAT IS **GOD.**

THE SUPREME THOUGHT IS **GOD.**

THE SUPREME WORD IS **GOD** that lives in humankind. **THE SUPREME WORD** IS **GOD** in human beings. Therefore, do not even venture to that area by saying 'I want to travel in spirit. I want to see **SPIRIT.** I want to hear **SPIRIT.** Or I travelled to the spirit land. I went to hear **THE SPIRIT.** I went to see **THE SPIRIT.'** That is so untrue! Pure lies! No human being, or angel or anything knows **THE SPIRIT.** If you knew **THE SPIRIT** by now you would follow **ME THE SPIRIT THE FATHER GOD.** Even Lucifer does not know **THE SPIRIT.**

The Holy Trinity

Lucifer was an **Object Self** that **I** projected as a **Mother's object self representing *'the negative utterances'*,** as a female daughter of **THE FATHER GOD** to keep 'there' to maintain the property as the house. And look at what she has done! Supposing Lucifer was a **Spirit,** she would have toppled **ME, THE SPIRIT** by now.

Lucifer is an Object Soul, as a supported energy! Her energy came from **MY "V-ME** as the female part of everything, **THE MOTHER GOD**! She is an object copy and **I** can call her back anytime into the WHOLE. The soul is a copy of the SPIRIT, and destroying the soul is like destroying your copy but **I** can imprison it. **I** can manipulate it! **I** can control it as **I** wish! That is why if you have a negative thought and you say, 'God forbid bad it', then that is the end of it. And so you can manipulate your negative thought. You can control your mind. You can control your thought, because if you allow your thoughts to control you, you are not a master of yourself. If you read **THE FATHER'S TALK (GOD PRESENT)** Lecture Revelation titled ***MASTERSHIP*** then you will know more about that.

All this struggles, preaching and teachings and sorting out problems on earth are because **I** want to make **MY POSITIVE SELF** in human form "WORD IN MAN" called Human-Gods to become **Masters of Themselves**. When you know yourself, you can know all things. And when you know all things you can know **THE FATHER GOD.** And when you know **THE FATHER GOD,** you give **ME MY** DUE GLORY! And then **I** will jolly-jolly up and down with you! *Saaih!* Wonderful!

That is **THE SPIRIT. I** do not want to dwell on that because **THE SPIRIT** is **Unhearable, Unseenable, Untouchable** and an **UNKNOWN ENTITY!**

B: **HEAVEN! UNKNOWN PLACE**

People talk about Heaven! Heaven! Heaven! You do not know the meaning of Heaven because you do not know **THE SPIRIT** as such you cannot know Heaven.

Nobody can visit Heaven! Nobody can visit **SPIRIT!** Don't allow anybody to fool you that you will go to Heaven! You are not going anywhere like that, Heaven mean the most perfect dwelling place for **ME THE FATHER GOD, HE IS THE SPIRIT** however, Heaven for humankind is the spiritual kingdom of **GOD** where love and peace reigns.

When **I** came to the world people asked **ME** how Heaven looked like. **I** told them that Heaven or Kingdom of God is within you. The more you look the less you see. Forget about struggling to go to Heaven, rather struggle to love one another, be a peacemaker, practice oneness and equality, have mercy and kindness for

The Holy Trinity

all human beings then you are in HEAVEN, not going to, you are IN.

That is why you can see that the soft light skinned human beings have developed fast by **The Mother Earth**. They are the **Basement in Creation** human beings in nature. **The Father and Mother Nature** grew them from **underneath** the earth as **"PARADISE OF SOULS"**. They are the **basement nature GOD LOWER KINGDOM OF THE PARADISE OF SOUL WORLD.** They are developed *quick-quick* to come and construct the world so that the physical life will be comfortable, but the carnal nature of the Mother earth siphoned everything from **ME THE FATHER GOD.** But now **I** have regained everything spiritually and physically back to **MY** SELF!

These people, the soft skin or light skin human beings that are a called "Whiteman", especially the so called scientists and other such intellectual thinkers of human beings think that they are very knowledgeable and so

The Holy Trinity

do not want to obey **ME THE SPIRIT.** They do not want to obey **THE FATHER GOD** because they believe that they cannot lay their hands on the **SPIRIT**. All what they concentrate on and study is how **THE SPIRIT** makes WATER. How **THE SPIRIT** makes BLOOD and how **THE SPIRIT** makes AIR. And they borrow the **air** and **water** and **blood** and formulate genes and create all types of negative and carnal things all over the place. What scientists are doing is called *okpokpok mbre, okpokpok mbre* compared to **MY DIVINE CREATIONS.**

Okpokpok mbre is original Hebrew spiritual language interpreted *mkpo mbre ntukeyen* (child play). *Okpokpok mbre – mkpo mbre ntukeyen* is children's toy. It is the toy that children make by themselves. Scientists are like children playing with makeshift toys they made by themselves.

The actions of scientists are as, for instance, when someone goes and

The Holy Trinity

cuts a **bamboo** and inserts strings from the roots of any plant to produce a make shift slipper or flip-flop. **Okpokpok mbre** is also like when the children carry a condemned car tyre or the wheel of a bicycle and attach a rope and pull it, mimicking the sound of a revving and moving car. 'Vroom-vroom-vroom'! They shout as they drag it along. These are the children driving a car. That is a nonsense car that they are driving! That is **mkpo mbre** (toy).

When people use plastic for make-believe-money as a caricature to play games with or do other things that is not actual money. Any counterfeit thing is **mkpo mbre** or **okpokpok mbre.** What scientists are doing and think that they are clever, but are infants at a, b, c – a, b, c, kwaghasikwak is **okpokpok mbre** !

Level O, they are toying about with **MY** natural and spiritual products as living creatures and living organism. **I** mean some of the scientists, the

The Holy Trinity

wicked ones. They are very, very stupid and nonsense type of human animals.

What scientists **I** mean the humble ones, should have done with the knowledge and wisdom **I** gave them to do things were to develop how to train people to love one another and how to make good and positive use of things like electricity that **I** gave them knowledge to invent. And also to use positively all the good things that **I, THE FATHER GOD** taught them to invent. But they left them! They have not even made use of all the good things that **I** have given them to do. They spend their time going out to try and create man and then go and live in another planet. They have crawled overboard!

Now, do you know what they are studying? As **I** mentioned before, they are studying how to make water. They are studying how to make blood. They are studying how to create air. Don't you know that if you did not invent an

The Holy Trinity

original idea and you do not want to improve through positivism, you improve by negative means and that means that you are causing confusion?

What Lucifer did in disguise is to give them the idea that they should get genes of cockroaches, genes of caterpillars, genes of monkeys and genes of many other animals and use them as potency for proteins and what they call vitamins A, B, C, D and so on. They mix all these things and give to human beings convincing them that with this, they will live long and live well and be very healthy. They also use the genes of animals to plant fruits and other food substances and call them Genetically Modified (GM) products. All that are satanic ways of contaminating the original things that **I THE FATHER GOD** has created. Most of the human beings that are positive know the hideousness of Genetically Modified (GM) products. That action is also

The Holy Trinity

another indirect means that Lucifer is trying to use to infuse the animal instincts in people to pollute the actual Human-Gods. That is exactly the aim of what those evil ones do.

When people eat these genetically modified products and give birth, the first thing that these sorts of human beings want to do is to be part of an army and go to war. So also are those who make these evil products because when they die and come back to the earth, they join armies to go to war.

What is the attribute of war? What does a warring character in someone mean? It means animal! Which living creatures fight one another? It is animals! Which creatures kill one another and eat each other? It is animals! Which living creatures destroy one another as well as themselves? It is the animals.

Ninety-five percent of human beings are animals. That is why there is no slightest peace on earth. The first thing a child born today learns is how to kill and how to destroy, how to be wicked, how to insult others.

Do you see any humility again on earth? All that you see on earth now is killing! All Killing! Killing! Killing! All over the whole world, the evil ones are using craftiness to introduce the human-animal blood into people so that they would be lots and lots of them, just as Lucifer is trying in different ways to bring dragons serpents and all other evil animals back on earth. That is what is going on now on earth.

She Lucifer or if you like, he Satan established this Valentine's Day to entice people to fornicate so that he would use that energy to make people manifest lots of animals on earth. Nevertheless, since **I, THE FATHER GOD** have exposed this secret all bad and negative spirit-souls have melted away! *Amen!*

And all will see. A GREAT UNIVERSAL CHANGE has taken effect

on earth and will make the whole world good from now upward, in the name and blood of Our Lord Jesus Christ. *Amen!*

The scientists per se are not really responsible for these creations from stupid and negative ideas that they try to implement. It is the same negative spirit-soul doing all that through them.

I, THE FATHER GOD I AM THE SCIENTIST!

I AM THE WISDOM!

I AM THE KNOWLEDGE!

But Satan hijacked them. He would enter into one person and such a person would have one stupid idea, 'Why can we not try to develop this', such a person would table it to the others and they would then form a union. When they form the union of "scientific research and technology", the members would focus on the NONSENSE IDEA to develop it and then the government will vote a lot of money to help them in developing the stupid ideas. And they forget what they should have done with the good talents **I** gave them and many other human beings on earth, which is to implement things for the positive benefit to the entire humanity. And to acknowledge that **I, THE FATHER GOD, I AM THE SUPREME SCIENTIST!** "OMNISCIENCE" **I** own this world!

I created this world and all human beings and everything seen and unseen. Look at electricity that **I** gave to the world for positive use. Look at aeroplanes for positive use. Look at cars of all forms and sizes that **I** provided including all other positive things **I** gave to humankind for positive use and all the good things **I** brought on earth to bring the world together, to bring oneness to the world, to bring love to the world. But the evil ones use these things in negative ways to destroy the earth.

They use aeroplanes to go to war. They use electricity to send rockets to kill people. They use **MY** good gifts to do all sorts of evil things! Is that what **I** gave them knowledge for? So, now! You have to make up your mind. You will decide which area you are going to operate and which area you are going to let go, because ***THE GREAT UNIVERSAL CHANGE*** is now in place to change everything for good and all negative things will be destroyed! In the Name and the power Blood of Our Lord Jesus Christ, *Amen!*

Heaven Is an Unknown Place. There is no place than THE HOLY SPIRIT OF TRUTH UPPER WISDOM and that is what is called Heaven. Heaven is within you. If you think well, speak well, hear well, see well and do well, you are with **THE FATHER GOD** in Heaven. That is all **I** give to humankind and any other object soul. Forget about any other ideological place you call Heaven. There is no place like that if you do not love each other and live in total peace. It is only **THE FATHER GOD THE SPIRIT** that is in **HEAVEN.**

Your HEAVEN is LOVE ONE ANOTHER. If you have PEACE, if you have LOVE, if you have all the good things and if you are a positive terrestrial nature then when you die that is, when you are physically here no more, **I** will call your soul a Holy Ghost. After seven generations **I** will use your ghost to make a Holy Angel that will go about to inspire people to do good things and live forever. But if you have not finished your generations, **I** will MAKE your soul a holy soul. You will come back and multiply all those good things on earth. That is what **I, THE FATHER GOD** does.

C: **UNHEARABLE IS THE SPIRIT.**

THE SPIRIT is UNHEARABLE. **I** have said this in so many **FATHER'S TALK (GOD PRESENT)** Lecture Revelations that **THE SPIRIT** is **Unhearable.** THE SPIRIT cannot be

The Holy Trinity

heard. No one can hear **THE SPIRIT**. It is only when **I** decide for you to hear **ME** then **I** will project **MYSELF** to **hearable** and then you can hear **ME**. **I** want this fact to be established, very well ingrained into people's mind, so that people will not be deceived when someone says 'I went to visit the Spirit... spirit sent me message to you. *Na* lie!

What Spirits do people hear? You only hear **MY** SUPREME SOUL, THE SUPREME WORD OF THE UNIVERSE THE CREATOR OF ALL SOUL "THE SUPREME THOUGHT OF OBJECTS SOUL CREATION". You hear either good or bad object souls or positive or negative object souls. You can hear the spirit-soul of Lucifer, the spirit-soul of serpent or the incarnated self of Cain all is through THE WORD.

You can also hear MY FIRST POSITIVE SELF FROM MY INNERSELF OF THE SUPREME SILENT THOUGHT.

The Holy Trinity

You can hear the spirit-soul of Abel, which is the positive one. You can hear the spirit-soul of Adam and all the positive prophets that manifested as natural Adam on earth. You can hear the spirit-soul of so many people. You can also hear the spirit-soul of negative spirit-souls. You can hear spirit-souls, but NOT **THE SPIRIT.**

When **THE SPIRIT** has not formed an object soul, you cannot hear that object. The first time you could hear an object is after **I** said "YAK" ("Let!") and "YAK" ("Let!") becomes the first pronouncement that the sound manifested physically on earth. So, "YAK" ("Let!") becomes hearable. The **Silent Thought** becomes **hearable.**

If there were no sound YAK ("Let!") there would not be a **Spoken Word**. And there would not be creations. So, **THE SPIRIT** is UNHEARABLE INDEFINABLE PHENOMENON.

The Holy Trinity

D: **UNSEENABLE**

THE SPIRIT is **UNSEENABLE**. **THE SPIRIT** is INDEFINABLE PHENOMENON **UNSEENABLE**. As **THE SPIRIT** cannot be heard then **THE SPIRIT** cannot be seen. Before **I** said "***YAK EDI***" "Let there be this!" **I** used **MY** sound energy GEN and then manifest voice with WORD "***YAK***" "Let!" then that creation became seen able via **That Spoken Word**.

So, without **The WORD** there would be no object creation. Therefore, do not say, 'I have seen **THE FATHER GOD** in spirit' when you don't know who **THE FATHER GOD** is. All the dreams you had and wake up to say you saw **THE FATHER GOD,** was an Object Soul in the form of human beings or Angels that represent **MY** SOUL. How do you see **ME** apart from when you see a human being like you as the image and likeness of **GOD? I AM** THE UNIVERSAL SUPREME WORD therefore, do you believe this WORD?.

The Holy Trinity

Everything is **THE FATHER GOD** but it depends on whether it is the positive side or the negative side. That is why The **THING** called **"THE FATHER"** is very deep. Then **I** Divined **MYSELF** to be **THE FATHER GOD,** so that when you see **THE FATHER GOD** area you would know that it is the GOOD side of **"THE FATHER."** Without that the TOTALITY OF EVERYTHING is **THE FATHER** because everything emanated from one **SPIRIT** called **ALLTHINGS, Unhearable** and **Hearable; Unseenable** and **Seen able; Untouchable** and **Touchable.** INDEFINABLE PHENOMENON is **HE IS THE SPIRIT; HE IS THE FATHER.** But when **I** say **FATHER GOD** as **I** say that now, it is **THE FATHER GOD! FATHER GOD! FATHER GOD!** Then, eventually when **I** have done everything, protected everything and sealed everything and projected **MYSELF** as **THE FATHER GOD** to physically manifest as **THE HOLY SPIRIT OF TRUTH**, then **I** have

The Holy Trinity

finished with all things. The next thing **I** will do after finishing everything is to switch off the light in the back, then the front alone will exist. The final switching off of the backlight is what people are waiting for. That is called the judgement day. The front forward, future will be light through out. And there will be no evil again on earth.

However, that cannot be done until every soul has been put straight to where they belong. And the blood of the condemned will be upon them.

Do not forget that everything is one. Be careful the way you treat others because those others could be you and you would not know.

E: **UNTOUCHABLE**

THE SPIRIT is **UNTOUCHABLE.** When you do not see anything then you cannot touch anything. This is the way **I AM** revealing **THE SPIRIT** before you allow anyone to deceive you. When you see anything in the dream, it is not **THE ACTUAL SPIRIT**. That is the Object Soul world. The things you see in the dream world already exist as objects and that is why you could see them in the dream.

The **Dream World** is a **Photocopy Basket**. The **Dream World** is an **Idea World**. Nonetheless, it is the **Original World** either from here or before here. From here means the object has already manifested physically and then went back to the **Object World** that is, **Soul world**. Before here means the **Object Souls** that have not yet manifested physically, but they exist in the **Idea World of DIVINE SILENT THOUGHT, THE SUPREME MEMORY OF THE FATHER GOD** where this information is kept. It is just like in the physical reality, you can have an idea as or an imagination of a creation but you have not produced your imagination or idea or the new creation yet.

The Holy Trinity

THE FATHER'S TALK (GOD PRESENT) Lecture Revelation is a **New Creation.** It is something that has not existed before in the minds of the people in this manner. Nonetheless, people hear about King Solomon. King Solomon! King Solomon! Everywhere, they read about King Solomon in the bible, but they never knew that in King Solomon there is a **Spiritual Library, "The Memory of THE FATHER GOD Library" THE GOD INFORMATION CENTRE** that **I** would bring out information and publish physically.

When **I** talk about **MICROSOFT AND BILL GATES**, they already exist in the **Object World.** The spirit-soul **HESIGNSTIN** means the spirit **I** used to put things in order, to correct things and **to secure things.** When evil wants to spoil something that **I** have not permitted, **I** disguise **MYSELF** and hide there in **MY HESIGNSTIN** to prevent it.

The Holy Trinity

I disguised **MYSELF** as a forerunner before **I** was born on earth as Our Lord Jesus Christ. And **I** made **MYSELF** to outwit Satan's evil scheme that when Jesus is born on earth he would not allow HIM to live. That he would kill HIM. When Satan's earlier plan failed, as he could not kill the infant Jesus, with that same idea he still demanded that Jesus be crucified. All the efforts of Satan to kill Our Lord Jesus Christ were that Christ had come to spoil things for her because she thought she was the chief controller of the world. But Satan did not know that the reason **I** accepted the death of Christ to occur was so that **I, THE FATHER GOD** would take the key of death from Satan and bring Light to the world of darkness and free all positive souls.

When light is brought to where there is darkness, then it means the world of darkness has changed forever for good. Now Jesus Christ is the Head of Hades and the Physical World.

The Holy Trinity

When Light was introduced to the place called darkness World, it was no more was Darkness World rather; it became the World of Light. If Lucifer knew that Jesus Christ was going to take light to the Hades and that her Queendom would collapse, she would not have allowed that to happen. **I, THE FATHER GOD** disguised **MYSELF** to achieve that. Do you see that? That is the Supreme wisdom of **THE FATHER GOD**?

So, the same disguise energy called ***HESIGNSTIN*** was what **I** created. And that energy in the current incarnation is **Bill Gates and Microsoft.** That **Microsoft** is the energy of **HESIGNSTIN** and **Bill Gates** is the incarnated angel soul that has manifested as "***HESIGNSTIN"*** who was born during that time of Jesus Christ as the disguised saviour of baby Jesus the positive thief. In essence, it was **I, THE FATHER GOD** that disguised **MYSELF** and came into the world as the angel ***HESIGNSTIN*** and become one of the two thieves that waylaid Mary and Joseph as they escaped with baby Jesus to Egypt. So, the angel **HESIGNSTIN** disguised himself then as a thief to save the Saviour of mankind.

Therefore, in an indirect way **I** was the copy of **MYSELF** in the form of that thief angel **HESIGNSTIN,** which is the physical **Bill Gates of Microsoft** at this present time. So, that spirit is **Microsoft** and that physical human being is **Bill Gates** put together. This is because of the promise **I** made to him then through **MY** Mother who said then that when my son would be in the Glory of His Father He would remember you. So, as **I** remembered **Bill Gates** now and **HESIGNSTIN** as **Microsoft** and put his name in the book of life nobody should be jealous. Even if Bill Gates is not happy about this, it does not matter. It is **MY** promise to him that **I** have fulfilled in the Name and the Blood of Our Lord Jesus Christ.

The Holy Trinity

There are so many copies of **Bill Gates.** In fact, there are millions of copies of him now enjoying in this world but some of them still misbehave. When they all receive their blessings, then **I** will put them aside.

If however, **Bill Gates** does not go forward from here, then, his good life and glory end here. What happens is that, when you have not completed your seven generations and you end in a bad way that means you have missed your blessing. But, if in your seventh generation you end well, then **I** will make you to be an angel again. And then **I** will continue to bless you.

As of now, the assignment for **Bill Gates** is to be the co-chairman for ***THE UNIVERSAL SUPREME WORD SEASON CELEBRATION*** on earth and promote the physical **WORD.** As he stands for the physical Word he must promote **THE SUPREME WORD OF THE UNIVERSE** by making the whole world to know what **THE**

WORD is. It is not in a negative way but in a positive way. HRM King Solomon David Jesse **ETE** will explain that to him.

Since **untouchable** became **touchable** via **THE WORD** then **I** have made you to understand that **THE SPIRIT** is **untouchable** until it forms it becomes touchable. Therefore, in all understanding, **THE SPIRIT IS UNTOUCHABLE.**

F: **SILENT THOUGHT**

This is what people do not understand, but you have to understand it now that **The Silent Thought of Creation,** is 'The **Supreme Thought'** that manifests all silent ideas through **The Universal Supreme Word,** which is The Supreme Life. Every **idea** is based on that **Silent Supreme Thought** until the idea becomes fruitful and is brought out by a physical human God, then each of those silent thoughts becomes an idea of event that people can see and touch. But when that thing is still in the idea mode that is, as a '**Silent Thought'**, no one can see and nobody touch, so, how then does this **Silent Thought** form the idea? It comes from '**THE SPIRIT**'.

I, THE SPIRIT is **The Thought Formula**. **I** manifested the **THOUGHT. I AM** the **THOUGHT – THE SILENT THOUGHT. THE THOUGHT** is the actual entity of the Soul. That is the imagination centre as is where '**ALLTHINGS**' as imagines and **IDEAS** come from and then those **IDEAS** are converted into '**THINGS**'.

G: **EXISTENCE**

Where do **the thoughts** come from? The **Thoughts** come from **EXISTENCE.**

EXISTENCE is **THE SPIRIT,** the actual **SPIRIT. It is "THE FORM"** that forms and yields **ITSELF**. This is where the **SELF** yields **HIMSELF**. The **SELF** multiplies **HIMSELF** by **HIS** Will called The Will of Nature, **THE SILENT SUPREME THOUGHT OF THE WILL OF NATURE**.

When **I, THE FATHER GOD** finished creating all the creations including the human beings, **I** allowed human beings to live by their will because they are small, small **ME,** as mini **Gods.** So, when you say the Will of **GOD**, the Will of **GOD** must be divine. Nothing that is not divined is the Will of **GOD**. **I AM** NOT a carnal Being. **I AM** not wicked. So, all positivisms are the will of **THE FATHER GOD.** And all negativisms are NOT **MY** will. That is from the negative side. You must understand this so that you understand everything. This is Part One of this Lecture Revelation.

THE HOLY TRINITY

PART THREE
THE MOTHER GOD, "THE SOUL"

A: **THE SOUL FORMATION**

As **I** explained before about **The Soul Formation**, is the multiplication of everything by **THE SUPREME THOUGHT.** This is the actual thing that made **THE MOTHER GOD'S** energy come to be.

I AM THE FATHER in all areas and covers everything, **Unhearable** and **hearable; Unseenable** and **seen able; untouchable** and **touchable.** It is the same thing with **THE MOTHER GOD** in all the physical creations.

THE MOTHER GOD is the first lower positive entity of **ME.** This is NOT Lucifer. This is the actual **hardware of THE FATHER GOD** that is represented by Water, just like the **software of THE FATHER GOD** is represented by **THE WORD** or the **AIR**.

The Supreme Air and **The Supreme Water** are spiritual super **Oxygen** and **Hydrogen** respectively. The **WORD** that resulted from between **THE FATHER** and **THE MOTHER** that is, the **AIR** and the **WATER** is called the SOUND. That Sound energy is called spiritual super **Nitrogen**.

Nitrogen is the Son "**ON**" LOVE 'THE ENO'. The Spiritual Super **Oxygen** and the **Hydrogen** as the "Father And Mother Energy" produced **Nitrogen**,

Nitrogen is the ingredient that **THE FATHER GOD** and **THE MOTHER GOD** brought out as THE WILL, the energy of oneness and through this, they brought out **Love**, and that is the **Love** that exists between **THE FATHER GOD** and **THE MOTHER GOD**. Therefore, between the **AIR** and the **WATER** is the **WORD** and that is the **Sound**, the

The Holy Trinity

Son, Love, *Eno* (Gift), 'ON' of nature.

When you have this wisdom and understanding, then you would know that **THE MOTHER GOD** is NOT **the mother** that is called EVIL. The one called evil is the representative of **THE MOTHER'S** lower energy, which is Lucifer the actual carnal energy of all the physical glory as things produced by **THE MOTHER** through **"THE LOWERSELF ENERGY"**.

The actual **POSITIVE MOTHER GOD** called **ABASI MU-UDIM "MY PLURAL SELF"** is a part of **MY** PROJECTED POSITIVE **SELF, THE SPIRIT SOUL. THE MOTHER GOD ABASI MU-UDIM** is the ONE that **I** use to solve so many problems as 'MYSELF WORKER'. Nonetheless, **I** represent every bit of **ME** with something. Every bit of **MY Thought** represents something so that none of **MY Thoughts** would be lost. For instance, if you have an inspirational thought and you did not write it down, then that thought might be lost if you do not remember it. Or another thought may come and override the previous thought you had, as you did not write it down as such, you will forget it. That is why anything you put down on paper, as THE WORD RECORDED will stay in the memory of the humanity, but in your own personal memory, you may lose it. Nonetheless, it is still there in the memory of the soul because you wrote it down.

SEVENTY-TWO MILLION **FATHER'S TALK (GOD PRESENT) Lecture Revelations** are the information **I** have decoded for KING SOLOMON SPIRITUAL LIBRARY. That is a lot of information. And it is everlasting information for all generations of humanity. **THE FATHER'S TALK (GOD PRESENT)** INFORMATION is eternal. It is for EVERLASTING LIFE.

Therefore, you! Human beings, if you learn to be humble you will understand things so that you would have the true wisdom of **THE**

The Holy Trinity

FATHER GOD that **I AM now** bringing out now on earth.

The **Sound** that came out from the generating force of **Water** and **Air** generates **Vapour, Mist** and **Energy** that brings out life physically on earth is **The Being as "the thing".** I instructed that every living organism and every living creature should admire, should love, should worship, should respect, should acknowledge, should appreciate and honour, **ME** because without that **BEING** there would be no physical life on earth. It is the maintenance between **THE FATHER GOD** and **THE MOTHER GOD.** That is what **I** call The Christ. And **I** presented that entity as a human being on earth as Adam. Every human being is a representative of that spirit soul but if you have turned to negativism then you lose that glory of representation. That representation glory is what the human being has as a gift through **THE HOLY SPIRIT** because **THE WORD** lives in you. Without that why should **I** talk now?

The Holy Trinity

This type of blessing is wonderful! You people that are witnessing this Lecture Revelation are so blessed. Anybody that reads this Lecture Revelation is so blessed because that is **ME THE FATHER GOD, THE HOLY TRINITY.**

I, THE SUPREME SPIRIT OF NATURE, THE SUPREME AIR, THE SUPREME WATER ... everything about this **SPIRIT** has come down to talk to mankind. By listening or even to having any sort of access to this information means you are blessed, unless you are negative. If you are positive you are well blessed.

Therefore, there is no amount of money and there is no amount of gifts that you would give to **ME** that would show enough thankfulness or measure up to this wonderful opportunity **I** that **AM** giving to mankind.

The Soul Formation started from when **I, THE SPIRIT** projected **MYSELF** and called that projection **Water,** which is the **Hardware** of the

The Holy Trinity

Air. As you know the **Air** cannot be seen. The sound of **Air** can be heard, but the **Air** cannot be touched, but **Water** can be touched. The whooshing sound of **Air** and the bubbling sound of the **Water** is the result of **"THE FORCE OF CREATION"** itself as it generates on top of the **Water.** But when that **Air** becomes very powerful then it becomes hurricane. When **I** put **MYSELF** together under that capacity, **I** destroy anything negative. **I** bulldoze them! You see this world? **I** can turn **MYSELF** and in just one second finish the world. And that manifests in **THE FATHER'S Angel** called **THE FATHER'S** Higher and lower Potencies. But that is not what we are going into now.

Human beings do not worry about offending **THE NATURE, THE FATHER GOD.** They would say **Mother Nature** did this. **Mother Nature** did that. They would not call **ME, THE FATHER GOD.** They only

The Holy Trinity

call **Mother Nature.** Do you see that? They do that because they do not want to give glory to **ME THE FATHER GOD.**

What is the meaning of **Mother Nature?**

MOTHER NATURE is **I, THE FATHER GOD** in a feminine form. All the physical things, heavy, kpum! Physical kpum!

"THERE" is **THE MOTHER.**

"HERE" is **the SON**

"EVERYWHERE" is **THE FATHER. And that is the TOTAL OF ME THE FATHER GOD, THE CREATOR OF THE UNIVERSE.**

But without EVERYWHERE there will be no HERE and there would be no THERE. Are you very, very brainless not to understand this? Where can you get a mother or son without the father? It is a very unintelligent thing for a woman to claim to be a single parent. Who told you a woman can be single parent? There is no woman that is a single parent. There are no

The Holy Trinity

parents without a man and a woman getting together to have a child. Even if you got the sperm from a tube, it is still from a man. You may be raising the child alone but you are not a single parent. You heard that the Virgin Mary got pregnant through the Power of the Holy Spirit and does means that The Holy Spirit as **ME** is **THE FATHER** of the baby. Supposed the Holy Spirit is a woman; would a woman get another woman pregnant? Tell **ME!** How will a woman get another woman pregnant? Answer **ME!** Answer the query!

 This is to tell you that the Holy Ghost Spirit-self was the male part that came to do what **HE** had to do with the female part to get her pregnant. **I** gave a Lecture Revelation on this in **THE WORLD THAT WAS TO BE – WINDOS AND WINIADOSA.** That was **MY** original plan. **I** did not create a woman for the carnality of man. **I** created Eve as **MY** own physical image copier **"the**

The Holy Trinity

womb of nature". And when **MY** divine energy would have come to Eve, **it** would have overshadowed her to have **MYSELF** born on earth. Then **I** would be a spiritual physical human while Adam would be continuing as a physical natural human. And the world would have been perfect. But Lucifer with her busybody quickly went to Eve and introduced nonsense into her before **I** came around to sorting that aspect of things out. That meant that indirectly Lucifer through the serpent went and had a negative idea with the wife of God who was Eve. That action and **MY** spoken word spoilt things till today. And look at how long it has taken **ME** to repair things.

Did **I** not come and die for it, to repair that? Therefore, no woman can get pregnant without the higher energy of the male part of her. Even if you stay one million years without meeting a man, you will die without being pregnant. Unless of course the woman goes to get pregnant through evil means, which **I, THE FATHER GOD,** do not permit.

All those who enter witchcraft, and secret society as well as those who believe in elementary things and speak negative words and do many other evil things, become frustrated souls for Satan to use when they die. What the evil ghosts, the negative and frustrated spirit souls do is that, they would surrounded any available person who is negative and practice evil and would inspire such a person to copulate with him or her when they have union with their partner. And when pregnancy ensues, it is their inspiration that produces the child. So, indirectly you have sired an evil child and that is what your wife or your partner will give birth to. That would mean that you are making babies for the evil one when you do not even have your own positive child. That is what evil and evil souls do and

The Holy Trinity

this is because Satan cannot have a child.

In a similar manner but positively where you have the Holy Spirit and the Holy Spirit inspires you, if you are a positive person doing good things, when you have union with your partner and have a child, then indirectly that influence of the Holy Spirit is what your wife would give birth to. That was what happened with the prophets of old.

John the Baptist for instance was a very highly spiritual child of Elizabeth. Who was the father of John the Baptist? What was his job? Zacharias was the father of John the Baptist. He lived in the temple and served **THE FATHER GOD** in a very high estate. And Elizabeth was also a very high estate spiritual person that knew **THE FATHER GOD** because she surrendered herself to the will of **GOD.** And that was why **THE SPIRIT** was on standby to bring forth the soul that was John the Baptist from them.

Therefore, if you are a child of **THE FATHER GOD** and from a respectable family then (your religion does not matter) the inspiration of **GOD** will influence the child you bring forth on earth.

Like always produce like.
A Hindu gives birth to a Hindu.
Christians give birth to Christians.
Judaists give birth to Judaists.
Muslims give birth to Muslims.
Buddhists give birth to Buddhists.

What you believe yields the energy for you to give birth to that. A Muslim will not go to be born in a Christian family especially as both religions are fighting each other. Christians fight with the Muslims and the Muslims fight with the Christians but they forget that they are from the same father.

If **I** want to pay you back the evil you have committed, **I** know exactly what to do because it is only **I THE FATHER GOD** knows the best way to pay you back in an exact measure for measure. That is why **I** say that thou shalt not join to fight the evil doer. Do NOT avenge any evil done to you. LEAVE VENGEANCE FOR GOD. Forgive one another.

People thought that Jesus Christ was a coward for preaching forgiveness. When **THE FATHER GOD** said to forgive and forget, it is for your own good. For instance, if someone does bad or evil thing to you and you pay the person back in the same coin that is, with same evil, you have progressed the evil as credit to your spiritual account. And you have also continued the evil because that evil you commit as vengeance will be added to the one done to you, then your evil deed becomes double to fellow you. You will then come back to this world born as part of that double evil and suffer for that. It means the continuity offspring of your evil will be following you about.

You cannot do away with the energy of the evil you have

The Holy Trinity

committed. It is your tank that is buried in your soul. It is your credit record that has been deposited into your spiritual bank account. Even if you die and your body melts to sand and your bones go to dust, your soul remains. The soul is the carbon copy of you that is not dead. When you die the body goes back to sand, the spirit comes back to **ME THE FATHER GOD** as **the Spoken Word** but the real you is your soul. It remains there in the air floating about, especially as you were doing wickedness to people. Any day it materializes, you materialize in a exactly the same thing, but in a physically disguised way. That is, you will look different physically but it is still you. Therefore, do not joke with **The Spoken Word.** Whenever the Word takes birth, that Word can never die again.

When someone dies without a child, particularly a man, people agitate that his offspring is lost. That is not true. Anybody that dies in this

The Holy Trinity

present incarnation and does not have a child will have the child or children you did not have hen you return. Your family is not lost at all. However, what would happen is that all the energy of the things you did including all the sins you committed or good things you do remain internally in your soul. Any day you close your eyes and die, the idea or ideas you had are packed together and kept aside for you as your records of life. When you take birth back into the world, you will come back with that idea or ideas and then spread them around as your family, they will come out from you and work in your favour. This is a very deep mystery **I** have revealed to you today.

The Soul Formation is **ME THE FATHER GOD. I AM** the one that formed and owns all **Spirit-Souls.** That is the hardware representing **THE MOTHER GOD.** When **I** formed **The Soul I** gave a Planet, a World, called **The Soul World.** People here dream there. The dreams that people have are in that world. That is the area that manipulates the **Thing** before the **Thing** comes to physical manifestation. So, that is the World of Incarnation. What you call Heaven is the World of Generation or blessed paradises. Both worlds are for **spirit-souls** and angels.

B: **SPIRITUAL WORLD OF SOUL OBJECT**

This **Spiritual World of Soul Object** is the exact thing **I** just explained above. When you have an idea about something, you have formed an imagination of that idea in your thoughts. And then you put the idea down on paper. If it is a construction idea, you write down the description of what you are going to construct so that you will remember your idea, but you have not yet constructed it. The idea is in the soul form therefore, you have already formed an object soul with the idea.

The Holy Trinity

If for instance, you had an idea to construct a car that has eight wheels instead of four, you would have imagined how to attach the wheels to the car. You then decide that the eight wheels would be attached in pairs to the body of the car. So, this description in your head or that you have written down on paper is the Idea World, as the Imagination World or the Soul World.

The day you actually translate that idea or imagination into physical reality by actually creating the eight-wheel car is when the manifestation takes place. If after creation, the car does not function well because that was your first attempt to experiment on your idea then you will stop producing that eight-wheel car. You would then keep aside that first product of your idea, as it did not function well. That first product could be kept in the museum. Or you could take pictures or photographs of that car and keep. It would then become an **Idea in the Object World.** It can

The Holy Trinity

never vanish for eternity in the idea world that there is an eight-wheel car but production of it was halted. Therefore, such a record will remain in the idea that there was an eight-wheel car once but it is no longer been produced.

You would forget about that for say one thousand years, which are decades and decades of generations, then one day, you will come back on earth with a higher understanding. You are the same person that had that original idea of an eight-wheeled car, now born into the earth as another engineer and you have improved now to a new Technology.

Now! You decide this time in your advanced idea, not to attach the wheels in pairs but to elongate the car and create a different eight-wheeled car whereby the eight wheels are attached singularly. That is, four on each side of the vehicle. So, you attach singular four wheels to one side of the vehicle and another

The Holy Trinity

singular four wheels on the other side instead of attaching them in pairs which was the case previously. That becomes the improved product of the same idea. That is how the Nature works and that is how the **Soul World** works.

With this, you can understand how **I, THE FATHER GOD** improves things, and also how **I** formulate things. And **I** put all these things in the **Spiritual World of Soul Objects.** That is the world that when you have a dream or when you are higher you can understand where you come from. But you are not in the **SPIRIT** WORLD. You are in the **Spiritual Soul Object World** where all idea formations are based. You should now understand and know that you are NOT in the **SPIRIT** World BUT in the **Spiritual Soul Object World.**

There are two dimensions of the soul. One of them is your heart and your mind. And the other is the

The Holy Trinity

Spiritual Object Soul World. However, all souls are based in the **Soul World.**

C: **MY PROJECTED SELF**

There was an idea in **ME**, from which **I Projected MY Seven Souls Objects.** These Seven Souls Objects represent the Seven Days of the Week. They are the **Gods of Creations**. When you read the Lecture Revelation called ***THE PARTICLES OF CREATION*** you will know more about this.

These Seven Super Soul human beings are the ones **I** use as **MYSELF**. These are **Seven Gods of Nature. I AM THE SPIRIT** that lives in them. One **SPIRIT,** which is **I, THE SPIRIT** lives in them and makes each of them a SUPER HUMAN GOD each time they manifest on earth. It started from Adam to Jesus Christ. Each time **I** come for a different assignment **I** use any one of these Spirit-Souls to come. And these Seven Spirits will support that person. And that is why nobody can fight against such a Super Human Soul manifest and win the fight.

Nobody was able to fight against Adam. Nobody could fight against Enoch, or Moses, Elijah or even Our Lord Jesus Christ and win. It is the same **Super Spirit Soul** that lives in them as the Natural Father. **I** have made so many inputs about this in so many of other **FATHER'S TALK (GOD PRESENT)** Lecture Revelations. So, when you read many **FATHER'S TALK (GOD PRESENT)** Lecture Revelations you will gain more knowledge about this. That is how **I Projected MYSELF** as THE SEVEN SPIRITS OF GOD that came in each generation to service the people in that generation as their FATHER. Each is the same Spirit as The Christ of God. They can bear any name but it is the same **SPIRIT, THE ANOINTED, THE CHRIST** that lives in them.

D: **THE ENERGY OF MY DIVINE IDEAS**

As **I** explained above, **The Energy Of My Divine Ideas** are all human beings called STARS, as the different talents of different people. All human beings on earth are Gods in Nature provided what is stored in them as the indwelling self is positive.

If you are a positive carpenter, an engineer or a medical doctor then these are **Divine Ideas** since they are handiworks intended for positivism. Therefore, from time after time such a carpenter, engineer and medical doctor will always be here on earth.

Let's say someone was a very good medical doctor or engineer in their previous manifestation on earth, then that person with the idea will always come to the world in a different advanced way and continue to improve. That is why you see that the world of today is more improved than the world of yesterday. And it is the same people that come back to improve on what they were doing because **MY DIVINE SELF** and **MY DIVINE IDEAS** are the Divine Talents. The STARS are the actual ideas that come to fruition into the world to improve the world. All the ideas are in human beings that are born and will be born on earth with these STARS in different capacities. Some human beings are bigger than other human beings in components in respect to ideas, assignments or talents that are in them. Therefore, you must respect one another and love one another.

If you kill someone, you are in trouble because you have killed one idea of **THE FATHER GOD.** That is why **I AM** not making peace of any sort with anybody that kills. You are to love one another. You should not kill. You should welcome all talents. Welcome all good ideas because all these good ideas around you are all from human beings. And they are all **MY** representatives.

How would **THE FATHER GOD** work? How will you see the Will of **GOD** and the Glory of **THE FATHER GOD** without humankind? How will **THE FATHER GOD** manifest **HIS** glory? As **I AM** talking now, **I AM** talking through human being. So, if **I** do not talk through a human being what then will **I** talk through being that the **SPIRIT** is **Unhearable.**

You cannot hear the **SPIRIT**.
You cannot see the **SPIRIT**.
You cannot touch the **SPIRIT**.

But you can hear the human being. You can see the human being and you can touch the human being. That is how **MY** glory manifests. That is why **I** do not joke with mankind because mankind is **MY** Glory. Mankind is **MY** home. Mankind is AMFAR-ONE - I AND MY FATHER ARE ONE.

The **SPIRIT** and the **WORD** both live in the SOUL and that SOUL is in the person which has manifested as a Human-God. That is what you should

The Holy Trinity

know believe. No human being and no amount of money can pay for this information. And this information will help many souls to improve for eternity.

E: **THE SUPREME MIND OF CREATION**

What is **The Supreme Mind of Creation? The Supreme Mind Of Creation** is **MY Silent Thought.** This **Supreme Mind Of Creation** is what **I** use to project the Seven super GODS, the Seven Flames of LIGHT of **THE FATHER GOD**. The Flames mean that one thing has circulated and multiplied to be seven in number. And that one-in-seven circulates and again multiplies to become seven-in-*Bringslion!* No one can count the number of human beings on earth and so the number is *Bringslion endless in counting!* And where did these *bringslion* of human beings come from? They all come from ONE human being, GOD THE FATHER ADAM.

The Holy Trinity

Each day of the seven days of the week stands for one type of spirit-soul. And each of these days materializes one talent of that spirit-soul of that day. Everyday has its own way. When today has passed tomorrow has its own way and so on to the seventh day and it starts again. That is the Seven Spirits of Creation that **I** projected from **MYSELF.** And these Spirit-Souls are Super Beings.

The Supreme Mind of Creation is **The Father** of all these Super Spirit-Souls. They are called the **Seven Spirits of God.**

I do not have just one Spirit –self because it is not a Spirit. The Seven Spirit-Selves are SUPER SOULS IN NATURE. **I AM** ONE **SPIRIT.** But if you ask someone a question with a seemingly obvious answer as, "How many Spirits does **THE FATHER GOD** have?" If the person answers that it is ONE, then the person has failed. Unless you understand that, **I AM THE HOLY SPIRIT.** If you equally understand that **I** projected **MYSELF**

to form the **Seven Spirits of Creation** then that means you understand that the SUPREME MIND OF **THE FATHER GOD** circulated **HIMSELF** into Seven Super Selves Souls that control the Seven Days of the Week. That means that each day has its assignment and represents **THE FATHER OF ALL CREATIONS.**

F: **THE INTERNAL SELF CREATIONS**

What is **Internal Self Creations?**
Internal Self Creation is the Idea that you have which **I** talked about earlier. That is, what you think of as an idea for something you want to produce but have not yet written it down.

Internal Self Creation is to think twice about anything you want to do. And that is **GOD** of your indwelling self. If your capacity of **Internal Self Creation** is thick and divine, then you would not make many mistakes in your life. Someone like HRM king

The Holy Trinity

Solomon David Jesse **ETE** whom **I** have given **MY** SPIRIT SELF of **Internal Self Creation** called, ***DECROMATICIAN Events* Creation** is quite a different person. It is the same spirit-self that **I** gave to his Father King David Jesse of old and it is the copy of that spirit soul that is Nelson Mandela, Barack Obama President of USA, Umaru Musa Yar' Adua, the President of Nigeria, Godswill Akpabio, Clinton of USA, Donald Duke of Calabar Nigeria and **Justus O. Mugbeh of BCS Nigeria.**

    I have given that same spirit-star to a lot of people not mentioned here that are positive.

    I have given that *Strainthen* spirit-soul to so many people but they swapped over to negativism. **I have** given this spirit-soul to Neil Kinnock of United Kingdom and many other positive human beings that think well about people. Their records are in **MY** hands spiritually. What is in them is the spirit-soul called *Strainthen* the **Internal Self Creation, Wealth**

Creation. These are the people that sit down and think thus 'what should I do to help people.' Look at someone like Bill Gates. He set up Charities to help people. It is not because he has lots of money. He could have used his money to sponsor politicians to go to war. But He does not use money to sponsor rubbish. Look another positive person called Richard Branson in the United Kingdom. He is the angel from the Water Planet called **SERAPHIM-MISHAM.**

Richard Branson is an angel from the **Water Planet** called **SERAPHIM-MISHAM**. He is a **Basement paradise in Creation.** He is the caretaker of mankind in a carnal way. He is the angel at Queen Sheba's Gate. In spirit-soul, he is paid one penny every second and this one penny per second he is paid in spirit-soul can materialize trillions and trillions of pounds. His wealth can never finish. He is an angel that is taking care of the Gate of Wealth and he cannot steal even a penny, but he is paid one penny per second and that is what has materialized Richard Branson's wealth physically. And his wealth is for the generality of everybody in the world. So, when this Lecture Revelation is transcribed and produced, A COPY SHOULD BE GIVEN TO RICHARD BRANSON.

I have the Records of every human soul on earth and **I** can decode all of them very accurately to reveal you exactly. These people **I** have revealed do not know themselves in this manner. If they go somewhere, maybe to a visionary, a soothsayer or clairvoyance or anyone of that sort to tell them about themselves, they are likely to be told rubbish about who they really are in a lower way. Visionaries, soothsayers and so on cannot tell them the actual origin of what they represent because **I** hide the true information about everyone in this world. There are many people who would puff up too much if they knew themselves.

If HRM King Solomon David Jesse **ETE** was a carnal person, He is the only person that can show-off too much in this world but if he did so, He would have failed. And that is because it is **I, THE FATHER GOD** operating in Him. If **I** do not reveal Him to you, you will never know Him. And you will not hear His voice.

As **I** was saying a penny, every second that Richard Branson is receiving in spirit will continue until he finishes his assignment on this earth. And he will continue to live like that. His physical wealth is not just for himself. That is, he cannot use that money just for himself. That is He must establish things that would benefit the entire humankind, which of course he is doing. And from this time that **I** have revealed this, his wealth will increase the more. He could even be richer than the government. He is a government of himself. People say he is everywhere and yes he is everywhere because his

The Holy Trinity

wealth energy comes from the natural wealth of nature, from the origin of water.

Bill Gates also is a government of himself, but the growth of his wealth has slowed down and **I** will tell you why this has happened. Bill Gates is supposed to be paid twelve pennies every second. That is what is supposed to be Bill Gates income in spirit-soul however, what has happened with Bill Gates is that he has defaulted. Forty percent of Microsoft defaulted and geared into carnality and negativism and became destroyed. That is why Bill Gates Microsoft is going down-down.

Negativism has entered into his energy self but not from himself alone. It is connected from many other companies. They use the Microsoft potency to create something that aids stealing because part of Microsoft's energy is imperfect. (He incurred that energy from the time of Christ as the good and kind thief that

The Holy Trinity

saved the baby Jesus). So, they steal ideas and develop lots of Microsoft technological products that are used for evil. They use such machines to send rockets and to kill people. So, the some of the idea of Microsoft swapped over to negativism. As a result, Bill Gates is no more paid twelve pennies a second. But when he started he was paid twelve pennies every second up to twelve years in spirit. Bill Gates himself is not negative but Satan and his negative cohorts have tapped a lot of energy from Bill Gates Microsoft to do a lot of rubbish on earth. But **I AM** going to correct that from now on. There are so many incidents like that.

As for Barack Obama the current American President, they are trying to use him. Evil is trying to use so many people to do negative things. But now that **I, THE FATHER GOD** have revealed this, **MY** positive children should be very careful. If you know that you stand for positivism, do not allow anyone to use you for anything negative. If they use you for negativism then your energy will be swap away to evil.

What happened to King Solomon in Israel before now? When **I** sent King Solomon to restore the Glory of **GOD**, as he is positive, the negative spirit went and used him and He swapped over. He swapped about thirty-five percent to negativism. And that affected the tribes of Israel but **I** have now restored it.

During the time of Rehoboam that thirty-five percent was the energy that operated and all sorts of things happened then. The kingdom split. The Romans took over and many other things happened. All that happen so that **I** would use King Solomon, to establish the United Kingdom. It was not supposed to be the kingdom of only Israelites. It was supposed to be the Kingdom of the whole world.

The Holy Trinity

I will repeat yet again, what **I** said in the Lecture Revelation **I** gave about Barack Obama, titled ***OBAMA THE STRAINTHEN - BARACK OBAMA'S SPIRITUAL ASSIGNMENT.***

President Barack Obama and his entourage, the positive groups of human beings **I** mentioned in that Lecture Revelation (HRM King Solomon David Jesse ETE knows all of them) are to establish PEACEMAKERS BODY- POSITIVE! POSITIVE! POSITIVE, to restore perfect peace on earth. Without that, the future of the world is bleak. This world as at now stands on one leg either to collapse or to stand for good. **I** delay action to destroy the world because Christ died to save the world. **I AM** therefore, rather saving the world through the name and the blood of Our Lord Jesus Christ. Without that the world would have finished by now.

Nonetheless, you have to know that the world will not end, but **I THE FATHER GOD** has **Twelve Lakes Of**

The Holy Trinity

Fire that **I** can put in place to consume this world whenever the people do not want to listen to **MY** voice. And all the disasters you see happening in the world is not yet the actual action. Any day that the actual action will start, everybody will shake with fear. Wherever you are, you will shake. But because of the prayers of the saints, **MY** positive children **I** have shortened the day. **I** will not allow it to happen for long. That day, you will see that the sky will come closer to this earth. You will not be able to find where to put yourself.

Let it be that **I, THE SUPREME SPIRIT OF ALL CREATIONS** forgive the whole inhabitants of the world and change them for good, so that the world would not see the disaster that has never ever been seen in this world of human kind.

Let the entire human kind listen to **MY** Voice and with trembling and repent! And stop going to war! And stop killing! And stop fighting! So that there will be Peace! So that there will be joy!

If **I** continue to hear the noises of bombs, the noises of bullets, the noises of war and the noises of problems then that will force **MY** action to take place. Stop the killing of innocent people!

This is the information on **The Energy That Generated The Internal Self Creation.** And **I** have mentioned the people **I** have given this energy. That is the talents that have something to do with the Divine **GOD** to people like David, Sampson and many others. **I** give the same energy to all positive people. They think positively and **I** work in them internally. **I** live in them as the tenant and they are **MY** houses.

G: **THE SEVEN SUPER SOULS**

The Seven Super Souls are to represent the Christ of **GOD**. After Our Lord Jesus Christ, the physical Jesus are the Seven Super Souls, the

The Holy Trinity

Natural Fathers. But the SPIRIT that lives in Jesus Christ is **I, THE SUPREME WORD, THE CHRIST OF GOD, THE ANOINTED ONE** and that is the one **I** call the KING of Kings and the LORD of Lords.

In this generation **I** come as **OLUMBA OLUMBA OBU, THE KING OF KINGS AND THE LORD OF LORDS**. It is the same Adam, the last Super Soul here on earth. If you like you believe and if you do not like, leave it!

Upon all the pregnancy of women and the giving of birth in this generation, the physical birth on earth of **THE HOLY SPIRIT OF TRUTH LEADER OLUMBA OLUMBA OBU** is the superlative of all births. **I, THE SPIRIT, THE FATHER GOD ALMIGHTY THE SUPREME WORD** manifested **MYSELF** physically on earth as **THE HOLY SPIRIT OF TRUTH LEADER OLUMBA OLUMBA OBU.** And **OLUMBA OLUMBA OBU** will continue to be One SUPER SOUL

The Holy Trinity

to represent Adam, **THE KING OF KINGS AND THE LORD OF LORDS** for eternity.

Every single human being born on earth, as a Human-God, human-animal, human-bird or human-fish, and whatever sort of human being you are, you MUST recognize this **Deity** and pay homage. You must know that The Centre Of Reconstruction, which is in The Centre Of The Earth that is Biakpan and Calabar in Nigeria, Africa where there is the original CENTRALIZED PHYSICAL FAMILY OF **GOD THE FATHER, GOD ALMIGHTY**, and **I THE SUPREME FATHER GOD ALMIGHTY** living as Christ, the **KING OF KINGS AND THE LORD OF LORDS. HE** manifested in **Biakpan**. All positive children of **THE FATHER GOD** must pay homage to **HIM**. It is not a church thing. It is not secret society. Just believe **HIM** and pay **HIM** homage and you are fine. This means that physically, **GOD PRESENT** is on earth.

The Holy Trinity

Then spiritually, physically and universally, the whole humanity as every single human being on earth MUST partake in ***THE UNIVERSAL SUPREME WORD SEASON CELEBRATION, ON THE FIRST OF OCTOBER TO TEN OF OCTOBER YEARLY FOR ETERNITY.*** No matter who you think you are, as long as you breathe the **Air, Have Life and Speak the Word**, you must join in that celebration. You must make yourself known that you celebrated **THE UNIVERSAL SUPREME WORD** during the season of the universal celebration. All governments of the land as families, groups in various forms and individuals MUST join in the universal celebration of **THE UNIVERSAL SUPREME WORD**, no matter who you are and what you may be. It has nothing to do with any such ideas as **I am a Muslim, a Christian or any kind of a Religion.** This is something to do with **ME THE FATHER GOD ALMIGHTY, THE CREATOR OF THE UNIVERSE AND**

The Holy Trinity

ALL MY CREATIONS, unless you can prove to **ME** that you are not **MY** creation then you are free not to join and celebrate **THE UNIVERSAL SUPREME WORD SEASON CELEBRATION.** If you would not join in *THE UNIVERSAL SUPREME WORD SEASON CELEBRATION* then you have singularly taken voluntary evolution to be oxymoron, as a disagreement person. And you will join Lucifer in Hell whether you believe it or not. Even if you are a holy person and you do not commit any sins, but you refuse to believe this then you are automatically Lucifer's partner. If any soul refuses to acknowledge *THE UNIVERSAL SUPREME WORD SEASON CELEBRATION*, you are automatically Lucifer's partner and you belong to that group, because that was what Lucifer did. She refused to acknowledge **THE UNIVERSAL SUPREME WORD** that **I** used for all creations. That is the only way that **I**

The Holy Trinity

can directly receive **MY** glory and enjoy the fruits of **MY** labour.

When you acknowledge and celebrate **THE UNIVERSAL SUPREME WORD**, then you are showing **ME** that you respect life because if Lucifer had accepted and celebrated **THE SUPREME WORD**, she would not go out to kill anybody or want to destroy anybody and she would not be a wicked spirit soul today. Therefore, if you refuse to celebrate **THE SUPREME WORD** by not partaking in *THE UNIVERSAL SUPREME WORD SEASON CELEBRATION* then it means you are wicked because you do not want to recognize **ME THE SUPREME WORD.** And **MY** soul will not be pleased with you! That is that for this one.

As the Seven Super Souls, **I** materialize as Christ or as the Natural Father or **THE SPIRITUAL FATHER** in each generation. However, in this last one **I** materialize as the **Spiritual** and **the Natural FATHER** that is,

Alpha and Omega in **One House** so that all the problems of human beings should solve for eternity, in the Name And Blood Of Our Lord Jesus Christ. Amen!

This part two ends here.

THE HOLY TRINITY

PART THREE
THE SON OF GOD THE UNIVERSAL SUPREME WORD

This part of **THE HOLY TRINITY** Lecture Revelation is very important. **I** talked about the **Seven Super Souls** but who lives in them? **The Son of God The Universal Supreme Word,** who is **The Total Energy of MYSELF** that materialized as a Human Being and lived amongst mankind, lives in all human beings. This section is to reveal the truth about the **TRINITY** so that you will not make any mistake. All these are ONE SPIRIT called *HE IS THE FATHER.*

A: **THE SPIRIT VOICE! THE SOUND OF CREATION**

As **I** revealed earlier, **I THE SPIRIT** is **Unhearable, Unseenable** and **Untouchable. I AM THE SUPREME O.** You can call **ME GAS** because, you cannot hear **ME**, you cannot see **ME** and you cannot touch **ME** but **I** fermented **MYSELF** and projected to be **dew** and formed the WATER.

WATER is **MY** hardware and it is the same thing as **O.** That is what you come to understand in your physics or chemistry classes or wherever you address such studies. You come to know that when you ferment the water or if you boil the water, the water will form dew and gradually evaporate and melt back to air. And the vapour that turned to dew will drop back and form water, which you can boil again and it will evaporate to be air and form water again. This action is continuous. That is **O.** That is the **Life Generating Force Of Energy** that produces life for all living organisms and all living creatures.

    This **Life Generating Force of Energy** is from **Supreme Air** and **Supreme Water.** They generate together and that energy then forms the **Sound of Creation** called **THE VOICE "YAK" OR "JAH" LET! –** Let! This be... Let! That be... When you read **HE IS THE FATHER** you will come across the full information of this revelation.

    That sound that brought out the complete meaningful **IDEAS** was because **I** engineered **MYSELF** until **I** had a meaningful **WORD**. When you beat a drum, people will just hear the sound of the drum *kpum kpum kpum kpum kpum kpum kpum! Kpum kpum kpum kpum kpum kpum kpum!* Howevre, all the sounds mean something in interpretation.
Remember this story about tortoise.

The Holy Trinity

When animals gathered together and wanted to have a festival of harvest, one of the entertainments in the program was a dancing competition. It was circulated to all animals that there was going to be animals dancing competition and that whichever animal danced the best and attracted the most audience would win the first and very prestigious prize.

Different animals have their different ways of dancing. Some animals dance jazz; some dance soul, some dance waltz, some dance reggae, some dance highlife, some dance samba and some dance their various cultural dances. They have so many, many dance moves. But the tortoise does not have any particular dance move.

So, the day arrived for the competition.

When reggae music was played tortoise did not dance. While all

The Holy Trinity

the other animals that danced reggae danced and danced, tortoise just sat there and did not stir. They played jazz and all the animals that dance jazz danced but tortoise would not dance. They played rap music and all the animals that dance to hip- hop danced but tortoise would not dance. They played soul, country music, waltz, samba ... name them and all the other animals danced to their choice of music, but tortoise did not dance to any of them. Tortoise just kept quiet while others danced and danced.

When they all finished dancing, they saw that tortoise still sat there and never got up to dance to any of the tunes of the music they played. They all knew tortoise. And so they asked tortoise what the matter was. 'Tortoise why did you not dance at all'? You know this is a festival competition and there is prize to

The Holy Trinity

be won. You are supposed to dance.' Tortoise said he would dance, but they should change how they played the music. They asked tortoise how you want your music to be played.

Tortoise said his music has no direction. That they should beat the drums randomly as well as haphazardly like kpughuru kpoogooroah! kpom kpom kpom kpugu rugu kpagaragah! kumo kumoo – just anyhow beating of the drums. It means dance, as you like, tortoise told them. Go right, go left, go forward, go backwards, stand in the middle and shake all over your body; dance not with breast and waist, but dance with hand, dance with leg and just dance anyway and anyhow you like. Dance as you like when you hear the beating of the drum. That is the interpretation of the music.

So, they started beating the drums randomly and haphazardly.

Then all the animals started dancing as they liked. Tortoise danced to the right and to the left; danced forward, danced backward, stood and danced with hands, with legs, stood on its head and danced and danced as the beating of drums say dance as you like. Then all the other animals joined tortoise and danced as they liked. Everywhere shook and was lively with the different and varied dance moves. Everybody danced as they liked and everybody was happy!

Tortoise won the dance competition because THE DANCE WAS FOR EVERYBODY – Dance As You Like. You see that? That is exactly what happens.

The physical creations of **THE FATHER GOD** materializes **wisdom, peace, love, harmony, equality** and everything via **The Spoken Word.** Yet people do not respect **THE WORD.** You speak, you write, you

The Holy Trinity

work and you manipulate many things with The WORD. You do everything by the WORD. **I** will explain and expatiate on this WORD and hammer, on it until every soul comes to this understanding.

There will be a time in this world and every other planet that as soon as you take an object soul or you are given birth to physically on earth, your duty will be to appreciate **THE WORD.** It will ring in the ears of everybody. **THE UNIVERSAL SUPREME WORD** MANIFESTATION with ***THE UNIVERSAL SUPREME WORD SEASON CELEBRATION*** will echo all over the place! – Whether you like it or not. This is the GREATEST CELEBRATION on earth that joins every soul together in unity, love, oneness and peace.

When you celebrate Christmas, Muslims have their reservations about that and so do not partake. Judaism sect does not partake either in the celebration of Christmas. All other

The Holy Trinity

religions make up a reason or reasons not to celebrate Christmas. Those who are born after Jesus Christ say they do not know **HIM** and so it is not their business. But with this particular program for the Universal Celebration of **THE UNIVERSAL SUPREME WORD** seasonally, tell **ME** who is not a witness of **THE WORD.**

Before you were born on earth, **THE WORD** existed. And you come to speak the WORD when you are born into the world. And **THE WORD** lives in you. So, you MUST celebrate **THE WORD** whether you like it or not. Do not say, 'oh I celebrate the birth of Jesus, Christmas and surely it is the same thing!' Do you see this Christmas people celebrate? It is a small celebration comparatively because **THE UNIVERSAL SUPREME WORD SEASON** CELEBRATION is universal.

__THE UNIVERSAL SUPREME WORD SEASON CELEBRATION__ is the biggest celebration of all celebrations. It means you celebrate **THE FATHER GOD THE SPIRIT, THE TOTALITY OF TOTALITIES,** your life and everything altogether. It means you celebrate the Word "ADAM", the Word "Abraham", the Word "ISAAC", the Word "ISHMAEL" and all the names that every human being on earth answers. This is even the only proper way to celebrate **THE CHRIST OF THE FATHER GOD**. With this celebration of **THE UNIVERSAL SUPREME WORD,**

Muslims will not have any words of excuse.

Judaist will not have any words of excuse.

Hindus' will not have words of excuse.

Buddhists will not have any words of excuse.

All those *cut-join, cut-join,* divisiveness, tribalism, segregations will end! From the day you start to celebrate **THE SUPREME WORD OF THE OF THE UNIVERSE** by partaking in **THE UNIVERSAL SUPREME**

The Holy Trinity

WORD SEASON CELEBRATION all divisions end. Through this the whole world becomes one flock with one shepherd.

THE WORD is your **FATHER**.
THE WORD is your **GOD**.
THE WORD is your **LIFE**.

If you refuse to celebrate **THE UNIVERSAL SUPREME WORD** during **THE WORD SEASON** that mean you have now taken evolution to condemn your life, whether you like it or not.

Those who celebrate during **THE UNIVERSAL SUPREME WORD SEASON CELEBRATION** automatically celebrate **ME THE FATHER GOD** in all capacities because **I AM THE WORD**.

B: "**YAK EDI**" **LET! I SAY.**

THE FIRST PRONOUNCEMENT I MADE is, **(YAK) LET!** So, **LET!** Is THE CHRIST that is the Commanding force, **LET!** is **THE KING OF KINGS AND THE LORD OF LORDS** thefore,

The Holy Trinity

if you call the **KING OF KINGS AND THE LORD OF LORDS, Father Let!** There is no problem there. That is what you say when you pray and start and end with "Let! Thanks and praises be given... It means that let all glory be given to **ME THE FATHER GOD** through Christ. But people do not understand it.

Let's be this! **Let's** be that! **Let's** not hurt one another! **Let's** have patience. You cannot say, 'let us kill because if you kill, you shall be killed.

'Let's go and fornicate.' Let's go and tell lies.' All that are negative and so you cannot use the command word for those sorts of things. But if you put **LET!** In every word that is positive you are blessed.

LET! Is the Command Word
LET! Is the first Son of God
LET! Is Akpan
LET! Is **Akpan Abasi** (First Son of God)

Let's be this! **Let's** be that! **Let's** do this! **Let's** do that which is good!

The Holy Trinity

Every positive thing starts with **Let!** And every negative thing starts with **don't!** That is stop! **Let's** be glorified! **Don't** be horrific! So, today, you have had the power of **Let! I THE SPIRIT AND ALL SOULS IN HEAVEN AND ON EARTH SAY "LET US JOIN TOGETHER AND CELEBRATE THE UNIVERSAL SUPREME WORD SEASON CELEBRATION IN THE NAME AND BLOOD OF OUR LORD JESUS CHRIST AMEN**

If you partake in ***THE UNIVERSAL SUPREME WORD SEASON CELEBRATION,*** then **I** will infuse the power into your tongue. So, when you say, **Let! I** will listen to you. As soon as you say **Let! I** will appear and solve whatever problem is bothering you for you wherever you are because **I** would have activated the energy of **Let!** - in you, being the first word of creations, if you acknowledge **THE SUPREME WORD OF THE UNIVERSE.**

C: **PHYSICAL CREATIONS**

I did **Physical creations** because of the power of **Let!** And the **Physical Creations** are the manifestations of **MY** glory on earth.

Therefore, as the **Spiritual Creations** are there to give the background to **MY** actual glory, all physical things also give background glory to **ME THE FATHER GOD.** Therefore, do not allow anybody to tell you that God is not physical, this and that. Who told you that **I THE SUPREME FATHER** is not all and all? What **I THE SUPREME FATHER** is NOT is negative. But anything that is positive whether physical or otherwise belongs to **ME THE FATHER GOD.** Do you want to tell **ME** that the physical house you live in is not positive and good? That the cars you travel easily from one point or location to another is not good? That aeroplane you fly with to very far and nearer distances is not good? That the ships you sail with on the seas are not good? Or that food that you eat is not good, unless of course you eat the food that is slaughtered, like eating flesh. That is not amongst the things that are good. But anything that you do that is positive, which is not against the will of **THE FATHER GOD,** is of **THE FATHER GOD.** That is the **Physical Creations** that bring glory to **ME THE FATHER GOD.**

All glory, all dominion, all majesty be given to the MOST EXALTED **SUPREME MAJESTY OF ME THE SUPREME FATHER ALMIGHTY GOD.** There is no other Kingdom apart from that of **THE FATHER GOD.** All the things that are positive are **HIS** agents.

Therefore, today is the day that all creations will not forget the Lecture Revelation of this day. And it will help many souls. And all positive human beings are blessed this day, in the name of Our Lord Jesus Christ. *Amen!*

D: MANIFESTATION OF MY FIRST PHYSICAL HOME

You can see the step-by-step movement of the Divine Will of **THE FATHER GOD.** From the Spirit **Voice, LET!** – came, the first manifestation of the **WORD.** Then physical creations took place. Thereafter, it was the manifestation of **MY** first physical home, which was Adam.

Adam was **God the Father. I** have to say this again. **I** said that **I** gave a Lecture Revelation that revealed the meaning of the letters **OOO** literally as the initials of **THE FATHER GOD. I** will reveal the letters of the Alphabets A to Z of which **I** have started with the letter 'A' titled *A OF A TO Z.* As **I** said, the magical secrets of **THE FATHER GOD'S** numbers are embedded in the Letters of the alphabets A to Z, which are twenty-seven letters and NOT twenty-six.

The letters of the alphabets are twenty-seven in numbers. And the numerals are ten that is from 0 and

The Holy Trinity

one to nine. If you do any other thing than that, you will find negativism within.

The New World counting starts from 0 to nine. Any amount of figures are gotten from there. In a very short time in the near future children would not be subjected to go through all the long, rigorous unnecessary complex counting. Just train the children on how to count from O, A to I, which is from 0, one to nine then they can add and subtract into *billions.* It does not need any other thing. That is the divine way of counting. And the numbers are written and counted in letters of the alphabets not in numeric form.

The New World Counting System are O, A, B, C, to I, which in the old system are 0, one, two, three, and so forth to nine. Therefore, 'I' is nine. Nine can also be written as OI. To write 'Ten' for instance in the new counting is AO. Counting AO that is, 'ten' is quite irrelevant. What is the point in counting ten when one has already taken care of that. Ten is one. Proper counting is from O to nine and again from O to nine. Therefore, in the New Counting System, numerals start from O, A, B, C, D ... to I (Zero, One, Two, Three, Four ... to Nine.) And then it starts again from O, A B... to I. That is **OOO** endlessly. That is how **I** count in spirit. That is why it is **OOO,** from O to NINE and back to O again and to NINE and again start from O to Nine and ten is AO. There is no ending to it.

The same thing with Alphabets, the counting starts from O, A, B, C, D, E ... to Z. That is **ZAKROLLS,** O A to Z and they total to twenty-seven alphabets, and that **The Completion.** Therefore, all is well in the manifestation of **MYSELF** in human home, Adam.

When **I** created Adam, Adam consisted of all creations on earth as a home, since every single creation is a spirit-soul. And all these spirit-souls are products of **MY** ideas. The

The Holy Trinity

greatest and the wisest of all things in spirit, soul and in the physical is **Wisdom.** And that is what **I** revealed as **W,** The **Wide Angle** that brings nearness to nearer people. That however, is not what we are talking about today.

Today, we are talking about the physical home. **MY** first physical home that **THE WORD** lived in was Adam that is why Adam is **THE KING OF KINGS AND THE LORD OF LORDS** from generation to generation. He is the first Father on earth.

Let **ME** ask you this question you who think you are clever. You, the philosopher, you the lawyer, accountant, President, Prime Minister, King, Queen, Church Leader and what have you, do you believe that the soul of the first man on earth is love? Do you at all believe that? Do you think that the soul of the first man does not exist anymore? You only know that Adam and Eve committed sin and that Satan deceived them and they

The Holy Trinity

committed that sin. What is the meaning of that?

As Satan deceived them and Christ came and died for them, did it not finished there. Did you not hear that **I** said, "It is finished!" on the cross?

Do you think that that Adam no longer exists? Adam is here. Therefore, you who claim to be a President, a Prime Minister, the in-charge of the whole world, do you not know that if you have not found out where Adam is, your father, your Father Adam, and you the child take over that position that you incur lots of problems? That is the problem of the whole world. That is the problems of the whole human race.

If you think you have juju as you go to bow down to an elementary spirit-soul to protect you, your problems are not over. You forget that there is one man on earth as the spirit-soul, tribe, and root that you have not acknowledged and paid homage to. When you do not bother to find your root, your original ancestor, your original Father Adam who is **God of the Earth,** then don't you know that you are finished? Pouring wine for your father that died will not help you. Calling the name of your father and your ancestors will not help you.

The libations that were poured by those of the ancient time not really for their fathers but for the first **Father Adam**, who they believed to be the **GOD,** they never saw. They invite him to join them and share with their bounties. When they eat anything they put some aside for Him. They believed that that Adam was somewhere. As you are enlightened now, you do not need to do all that. Just have the belief in your heart and love one another.

That first soul multiplies to result you, therefore you are one of the results of the multiplication of Adam. So, why don't you love everybody? That is all that **I** need from you.

The Holy Trinity

Do NOT plan evil.
Do NOT plan any wickedness.
Do NOT hate anybody.

You MUST recognize that **I** have now revealed that the first man, Adam, he is now on earth. **I THE SPOKEN WORD, I THE SPIRIT** that is giving this message, came to establish that ADAM, OLUMBA OLUMBA OBU, THE UNIVERSAL SHRINE, THE FIRST AND THE LAST ADAM. THE NATURAL FATHER AND SPIRITUAL FATHER ARE IN ONE HOUSE NOW ON EARTH, HE IS THE KING OF KINGS AND THE LORD OF LORDS.

If you like start your life from there, if you don't like to, then, don't bother, but one truth remains as an everlasting truth, is THAT THE TRUTH IS AN UNCHANGEABLE NATURE, in the name and blood of Our Lord Jesus Christ. Amen!

E: **THE WORLD OF THE SPOKEN WORD**

The World of the Spoken Word is every human being. But where do these human beings live? They live hear on earth. So, this earth, this world that you live in, do you think it is an ordinary place? This earth is a spiritual planet called THE WORLD OF MANIFESTATIONS and every human being is a spirit soul, which means the house of life and that is THE WORD.

Are you not moving around? Are you not talking? You are the quickening object soul. And what is quickening in you is the **WORD** that is quickening your system. Do you see that? So, this particular world you are living in is so very much expensive and positive than the Hades.

Hades is where if you want to borrow a **Second Hand Spirit-soul**, you go to. People like soothsayers, magicians, clairvoyants go there and borrow the spirit-soul of people **I**

The Holy Trinity

refuse them entry back to the **Safe Side Area in MYSELF.**

When you come to this world and you commit evil and you die, **I** ban your spirit-soul not to come to the **Safe Side Area** and you then roam about. **I** revealed that in the Lecture Revelation titled ***THE ROAM ABOUT SOULS THE FRUSTRATED SOULS.*** When you pour libation they would come to drink that because they do not have access to the place that is the **Destination.** And so they hang around. Those are the souls that when you offer a little sacrifice they come and talk and give you second hand information. They become intermediary spirit-souls that work for people as slaves but you cannot command the spirit-soul of a good human being that has died. Do you think it is everybody that you can command? You will not even see them in your dream

Do you know what Satan does? It is really very funny to see someone like a President of a country fall victim to this. A Prime Minister, a King, a Queen and all the rich and prominent people in the world become slaves to small, small souls that died some years back.

Do you know what obtains? Someone manipulates those souls that were people that died and asks you to come and register your name for you to be protected. When you do, you have taken what is called **evil soul credit.** You forget that as you accept that evil protection you have taken **evil soul credit** to pay back when you die.

When you take the evil soul credit, it is a debt you must pay back. If you go anybody that goes to another person and ask for help and the person gives you a talisman or gives you anything to wear on you or hang on you or in your house as a form of protection or the person initiates you into secret society to protect you, it means you have taken **evil soul credit.**

Evil soul credit means that as those souls are helping you, you owe them and when you die no matter how prominent and very important you may have been here, you are going to be a slave to others. They will order you about. That indeed, is a very pitiful thing to see someone like you, someone as prominent and important as you are the **image** and **likeness** of **GOD**, become a slave to someone else that died years before and has became an evil spirit soul manipulated by soothsayers. And when you die and serve others, as you have become a slave that is ordered about, that increases your evil the more. As a result the whole world becomes full of evil.

As for **ME THE FATHER GOD, I AM** waiting for the day that **I** will destroy all of them in the lake of fire. Therefore, as **I AM** giving this Lecture Revelation **I AM** giving the remedy to save your souls because **I** will destroy those evil souls.

When **I** destroy those evil souls there will be no bad dreams again because those evil soul agents that are working for Satan to disturb people will be no more. What they do is that they are working as evil agents to get more and more credits to survive. When **I** destroy them there is no more evil operations. It is just like the evil agents in the financial companies or evil banks in this mundane world are operating.

When the government puts money in the bank or when people get rich through the businesses they do or even earn an income through working, the banks would encourage them not to spend the money but to save it. People then leave their money in the banks and the banks trade with the money irresponsibly. They would not allow proper circulation of the money to all the people on earth. They sideline some people by refusing them some capital and give huge amounts of money to some others. And now they have problems, global

The Holy Trinity

economic crises. The whole world has huge economic problems as **I** have imprisoned all the money. People of the world have not seen anything yet. Go to heaven and come back you will not escape this mess you have created in the world as you call it "economic crunch or economic downturn".

The world will see more economic problems because that is the catastrophe that the evil financial institutions and their architects are causing on earth as they refuse to allow the wealth of **THE FATHER GOD** to also spread to the poor and needy all over the world.

The people of the world share the money that is for everybody in the world to just a select few. You spend money on nuclear weapons and all other war implements as well as non-profitable space projects and many other wasteful economic projects. So, as some select few carve out the global finance that is for everybody in the whole world for themselves, they are *quating* (squatting) the global economy and they are *quating* the world. They put the world in their palms and control the world. What **I** will do now is to destroy those palms and set the world free. The evil financial architects are also in trouble.

Therefore when you accept the protection from the evil spirit-souls you have accrued Evil Soul Credit. The evil energy serves through talisman, secret societies and many other elementary set ups. There are people who manipulate these evil spirit-souls and offer sacrifices to them therefore, when you are involved with these sorts of evil people by accepting their protection, you are also involved with offering sacrifices. Even if you don't offer the sacrifices by yourself, you pay a hell lot of money to them to offer sacrifices to the evil spirit-souls on your behalf. You are therefore polluting the world with your evil practices.

All these Records are in **The Spiritual Library** that **I THE FATHER GOD** keeps. Angels keep the records of everybody on earth in **The Spiritual Library of THE FATHER GOD. I AM** now decoding and revealing some of this information and making them available to the whole world.

Therefore, stop evil! Stop killing! Stop all these evil activities you are involved in and with. If for instance you are in the army, you are involved with killing. And if you die as an army person, you will be born back on earth to eventually become an evil soul army thus spoiling the world the more. So, let the world change for good through practical positivism.

The Holy Trinity

F: WHO OWNS THE WORLD AND THE CREATIONS

Ask yourself this – 'how did I come to be in this world? My mother gave birth to me and I was very tiny. How did that come to be? Today, the people of the whole world should ask themselves this question – **Who Owns This World And The Creations?** If they don't know, they should say so.

People have seen this big thing called **The World.** At least those here in London have seen this part of the sky, how much more extending your sighting to the continent of Africa. You cannot even cover that. Yet nobody sits down and really asks, **Who Owns This World And The Entire Creations.** Is it not somebody, a **SPIRIT,** a Phenomenon that owns this wonderful property, big premises like this world? Yet people carve out areas of the world and claim ownership and **I, THE FATHER GOD** keeps quiet. 'Oh I am this! Oh I am

The Holy Trinity

that!' But when you die you go down six feet into the earth. So, for the children of **THE FATHER GOD,** the first wisdom is for you to tremble, for you to fear. It is not fear like evil fear but to have respect, reverence about **ME THE FATHER GOD,** THE **OWNER** OF THE WHOLE WORLD.

When **I** created the world, the echo everywhere was, oh everything is nice! The terrestrial realm is beautiful! All the components of **MYSELF** exclaimed that everything is good! **I** said, is that so? Okay let **ME** send the spiritual people from Heaven to the earth to see whether they really understand love. But Lucifer failed woefully with her group of rebellious angels, that have turned out to be evils and demons today. So, what is it that is good about failure and being a rebel and evil? Evil is **'cast and ban'** from everywhere. A small child with the Holy Spirit easily **cast and ban** evil. Therefore, it is not a good thing at all to be negative.

The same thing that happened before is happening now. **I** have brought the same test on earth now. And people said all sorts of things then and are still saying all sorts of things today against **THE SOLE SPIRITUAL HEAD OF THE UNIVERSE.** People say all sorts of things against **THE SUPREME WORD OF THE UNIVERSE** that has manifested physically on earth. What is two thousand years? It has come round again. Is it not the same thing that happened two thousand years ago when people then did not believe that JESUS CHRIST IS THE SON OF GOD AND THE OWNER OF THE WORLD. The same thing is happening now.

How many people believe that every two thousand years **I THE FATHER GOD THE SUPREME WORD OF THE UNIVERSE** comes to inspect the world and save the positive children of God? Does it then mean that from the time of Adam or the

The Holy Trinity

time of Our Lord Jesus Christ till now that **I** will not come to **MY** world? **I THE FATHER GOD** have been here physically in the world a while now and have finished **MY** work before the year Two Thousand. The year Nineteen Ninety-nine was when **I** finished **MY** work.

I AM here again on this earth physically since Nineteen Eighteen. From Nineteen Eighteen to the year Two Thousand was the period **I** worked and finished everything and reconstructed the whole world and **I** set out things to do here on earth spiritually and physically. Now **I AM** testifying about the work **I** did. Becuase **I** have put things in place spiritually. Now, it is **THE GREAT CHANGE** that will be unveiling every day. The events you will hear and what you will see, no ears have ever heard and no eyes have ever seen and none has even written about it anywhere yet in the world. Watch and see. But blessed are those who have

The Holy Trinity

not seen but they believe because they will save their soul.

G: **I THE FATHER GOD I AM THE WORD**

I, THE FATHER GOD I AM the WORD you are hearing now. Don't look for **ME** by deciding 'oh, I should travel to go see **THE WORD.**
THE WORD is right inside your heart.
THE WORD is in your name
THE WORD is in your body
THE WORD is in front of your atmosphere talking to you and you answer. You should reason with **ME.**

The components and way **I** created humankind is very wonderful. Every human being is a computer. **I AM the Network.** And **THE WORD** that manipulates the computer is the computer software. So, when you are born on earth as a living soul, the **WORD** operating inside you is linked back to **THE SUPREME SPIRIT.** And everything that you do is linked by

The Holy Trinity

the **WORD** back to **THE SUPREME SPIRIT** because that **WORD** is your thoughts. Your heart is the hard disk that stores the capacity of memory from when you are conceived to when you die. All that records are there. So there is no way you can escape! This is what **I** revealed **Microsoft** in the Lecture Revelation titled ***THE SPIRIT OF BILL GATES (BILL GATES AND THE MICROSOFT)*** but people do not understand. But when you read this Lecture Revelation and the one on **BILL GATES** and compare them you would know that **I AM THE SPIRITUAL COMPUTER AND MANUFACTURER** and that EVERY HUMAN BEING IS A COMPUTER SOUL.

The palms of your two hands are monitors just like the computer monitor. Your face is a projector of light and your heart is the hard disk. You have internal memory that is inbuilt in you. The inbuilt memory of everybody is not the same capacity. There are lots of memory capacities in some people and less in others.

The Holy Trinity

Somebody like HRM King Solomon David Jesse **ETE** has **Unlimited Comprehensive Memory.** There are so many people like that.

You! Who does not believe **ME THE FATHER GOD** that **I AM THE FATHER'S TALK GOD PRESENT** you are in trouble because everything you do is recorded. When you are not operating according to the instructions that are stored in you and you do something else that means you have changed the make. You have borrowed that something else that you are doing. That is how you are in trouble. Therefore, **I AM** advising the entirety of human beings to surrender to **The Supreme Network,** which is the new Adam, **the Universal Leader, the Universal Sole Spiritual Administrator Head of All Human Beings, the Christ of God on earth** who co-ordinates every human being. Nonetheless, that **Network** is stored in you. It is **The Spirit.** It is **The Spoken Word.**

Therefore when you partake in **THE UNIVERSAL SUPREME WORD SEASON CELEBRATION** then it means you have signed on to this Super Network of **THE FATHER GOD,** which is the Holy Spirit to correct you. And then you will be a part of **THE SUPREME FUTURE.** And destruction will not reach your soul.

That is what **I** have for you in this part of this **THE HOLY TRINITY**.

PART FOUR
CONCLUSION

A: **THE HOLY SPIRIT OF TRUTH IS THE TRINITY GOD**

THE HOLY SPIRIT OF TRUTH IS THE TRINITY GOD. I will use this part to summarize the whole Lecture Revelation of today. **The Holy Spirit Of Truth Is THE TRINITY GOD** that has manifested physically. **HE** is the last Personified **WORD** on Earth that has brought the first Adam back on earth as the Natural Father. **The Holy**

The Holy Trinity

Spirit HIMSELF Personified is THE FATHER GOD who personified as **THE TRINITY** which is **THE FATHER, SON** and **THE HOLY SPIRIT.** That is why **I** said that **I, THE FATHER GOD,** never changes. **I AM** SINGLE. **I AM** ONE.

The Holy Spirit Of Truth is **THE TRINITY GOD. HE** is the completion of everything. **HE** is **THE FATHER GOD. HE** is everything. **THE FATHER GOD, THE MOTHER** and **THE HOLY SPIRIT** altogether as a family are ONE. That is why **I** finally and ultimately brought back The Brotherhood. **I** returned the lost Brotherhood. **I** brought it back for humankind. And that is the Kingdom of God because that is where the King of Kings and the Lord of Lords is the Head.

It does not cost you anything to humble yourself and accept this. It will not take away your pride. It will not take away your glory. It will not take away who you are, whether you

The Holy Trinity

are a politician, a president and so on. Whatsoever you are, it will not take it away. A father does not take away his son's glory. Rather you the son are promoting your father's glory.

All you need to do if you are positive is to pay homage and believe and celebrate during **THE UNIVERSAL SUPREME WORD SEASON CELEBRATION** and promote your **GOD** FATHER THE ADAM AND NEW EVE. When you read the Lecture Revelation titled: ***ESIEN EMANA AKPAN THE AFRICAN PROBLEM; THE NIGERIA IN AFRICA*** you will know this.

I want the whole world to know that it is not by pride or by glory or anything. It is natural. Africa was the first port of creation on earth. The first word "**YAK**" "**Let!**" – was pronounced in Africa. Therefore, Africa is the senior soul land on earth. You have to take the lead. You have to put in a hand of support. Take it as your parents. If you move away from

The Holy Trinity

your parents and eventually you become rich and your parents are not negative then you have to support and promote them.

Previously Africa was negative through worshipping idols and did all sorts of traditional things as though they were children. Their behaviours then, were like children. They had shrines and all such things because they were ignorant. Now **I, THE FATHER GOD** have come back to show them how **I** was. Now they will take in the proper mode of worship. Some people still argue that we should not worship human beings but they themselves are worshipping wood, stick, mould image, stone, and even animals. Do you see human beings with stupidity? You worship stone that cannot talk. You order talisman from India. You become a slave to all those things that cannot see, cannot hear and cannot speak, as they have no voice. But look at the Advanced Gods as human beings who are the Advanced Gods because they are Gods of intelligence. Human beings are the houses of **THE FATHER GOD.** When you ask, 'who human beings to worship then that means you are very stupid because human beings give food. Human beings give birth to humankind and physically facilitate the growth of mankind. Wood cannot give birth much more to born a human being. Animals cannot give birth to a human being.

Look at you! Stupid human-animal! **I** call you stupid because you are stupid in the nature of your being human animal. How can you a human being who can speak well, go back and bow down to a stone or wood that does not speak; bow down to take talisman – a piece of say gold and put in your hand to protect you. It sounds so difficult to believe! It sounds so unreal!

You are not real. You are like artificial flower or any artificial thing.

The Holy Trinity

That is why you are doing what you are doing and worshipping idols. If you were really a human being with sense, you would reason that instead of believing in something that cannot speak or hear you should believe in humankind that can speak and can hear.

Mankind can speak to spirit-souls. If you cannot speak to spirit-souls then you cannot speak to a human being like you. If it were not so then why can you speak at all?

People ask, 'oh how can you worship a human being. They should worship what? **I** created humankind in **MY** image and likeness. So, if you respect a human being, you respect **ME THE FATHER GOD.** If you respect your father then you respect **God The Father.** If you respect your mother you respect all **GODS**. Therefore that type of stupidity has passed. **I** have come back now to speak with reasonable human beings that have intelligence. If you think you are a

The Holy Trinity

human being, I mean a proper human being, then you will understand this WORD.

You have known today that **THE HOLY SPIRIT OF TRUTH IS THE TRINITY GOD.**

B: **I THE FATHER GOD I AM THE SPIRIT**

I, THE FATHER GOD I AM THE SPIRIT. THE SPIRIT can turn **HIMSELF** to be anything. Therefore, you hear that **SPIRIT** is Unhearable, Unseenable, Untouchable and has now become hearable, seen able and touchable. So, **SPIRIT** can be anything!

The only phenomenon that turns into anything is **THE SPIRIT. Spirit** can enter into you and act and you would think you are the one doing what you are doing. **Spirit** can do anything! In that regard **I** don't need anyone to judge another for **ME THE FATHER GOD. I** don't need anybody to direct for **ME.**

The Holy Trinity

I AM THE SPIRIT. I know what to do with everybody. Those who will listen to **ME THE FATHER GOD, I** know what to do with them and those who give a deaf ear to **ME** (as long as you have come across this information and you deny it) **I** know exactly what to do with you.

However, it is **MY** Will that you spread this information as far and wide as possible around the whole wide world. Not just this particular Lecture Revelation but also other **FATHER' TALK (GOD PRESENT)** Lecture Revelations as well as **THE EVERLASTING GOSPEL OF THE HOLY SPIRIT OF TRUTH.**

Tell the people that **THE FATHER GOD ALMIGHTY, THE HOLY SPIRIT OF TRUTH** has manifested physically into the world as the NATURAL and SPIRITUAL Adam and BROTHERHOOD OF THE CROSS AND STAR is THE NEW JERUSALEM, THE CITY OF THE CHILDREN OF GOD. BROTHERHOOD OF THE CROSS AND STAR is NOT a church; it is a **NEW KINGDOM OF GOD**.

I have no business with religion or with churches. But **I** have everything to do with Human beings that have LOVE because BROTHERHOOD IS ONE FAMILY OF THE SAME PARENTS therefore, understand that it is universal, then you will be okay.

When you introduce **ME THE FATHER GOD** to people in the above manner and any such person or persons refuse to accept **ME, THE SUPREME SPIRIT THE FATHER GOD ALMIGHTY THE SUPREME WORD THE CREATOR OF THE UNIVERSE, I** know what to do with them when the time approaches for **ME** to react.

C: **I THE FATHER GOD I AM THE SOUL**

I AM THE SOUL OF EVERYTHING. Don't forget that **THE SPIRIT** made **Objects Souls** and the object souls manifest physically.

Every object soul is part and parcels of **ME THE FATHER GOD.** So, there is no way you can escape **ME**. Don't forget this truth.

D: I THE FATHER GOD I AM ALSO THE PHYSICAL HUMAN BEING

Don't forget that because these **Object souls** have turned out to be human beings then **I, THE FATHER GOD I AM** also the physical human being. So, if you respect any humankind being, you respect **ME.** If you love mankind, you love **ME THE FATHER GOD.** Any good thing you do to a human being, you do it to **ME THE FATHER GOD.** And that is why you shall reap exactly what you sow.

E: I THE FATHER GOD I AM THE SUPREME WORD THAT LIVES IN EVERY LIVING CREATURE AND EVERY LIVING ORGANISM

I live as the **Spirit of Life** in every living creature and every living

The Holy Trinity

organism to make them to be alive. That is why if any human being cuts down a tree and carves something out of it or uses any object for that matter and speaks the WORD into that thing, then that thing yields energy. The power that you infuse into that thing that you believe is the power that came out from a living human being which is God.

Without a living human being ghost cannot be invited. You must be a living person to invite any ghost. You must be a living human being to invite any spirit-soul object to come and act. Without that it will not act. Don't allow anyone to tell you that Satan did this Satan did that. Without the human being inviting anything called Satan he would not act because the WORD must speak. Because you are god, you must have invited Satan. You must do something before something works. The WORD is the cause of everything that happens on the earth via the human being. But **I THE**

FATHER GOD is the activator of every human being.

F: I THE FATHER GOD IS ALL AND ALL AND IN ALL THINGS BROTHERHOOD

This summarizes everything. **THE SPIRIT IS EVERYTHING. I THE FATHER GOD I AM ALL AND ALL** and **I LIVE IN ALL THINGS** that materialize Brotherhood. Everything in Heaven and Earth put together means Brotherhood, one Family of the same **FATHER GOD.** That is Brotherhood. That is not something anybody should argue about if you are a reasonable person.

This does not need preaching. The only need is for you to love and know as you know now and agree with the whole thing and say 'let me accept that am one of the family members of the whole universe Brotherhood.'

G: **I AM THE HOLY TRINITY THE SUM TOTAL OF ALL QUALITIES OF MANNERS OF LIFE**

This is where **I** round up the whole matter. **I AM THE HOLY TRINITY.** Do not forget that **THE HOLY TRINITY** that **I AM** talking about manifests physically in you and every human being.

I revealed **THE TRINITY** in Heaven, **THE TRINITY** on earth and **THE TRINITY** in the soul. **The Trinity** on earth is the human being. In human beings you will see **The Spoken Word**, as LIFE. **The Spirit** is **Life** that engineers the words that you speak. **The Spirit** is the breathe of life. Your physical body contains the **Spirit,** the **Blood** and the **Water.** That makes you a house of **THE FATHER GOD** representation on earth. You are gods on earth. That is Adam in a small way. But your physical Father Adam is still on earth.

Therefore, every man is Adam and every woman is Eve. That is why you must NOT kill anybody. You must NOT hate anybody.

You should love.

You should have mercy.

You should have patience.

You must be peaceful with everybody.

You must treat everybody kindly.

You must be humble with everybody.

You must respect everybody as you respect yourself.

Think well. Speak well. See well, hear well and do well.

This is the order **I** give today for the understanding about **THE TRINITY GOD.**

And believe that you are respectful to **THE FATHER GOD.** If somebody respects you the person respects **THE FATHER GOD.** And if you respect someone you are respecting **THE FATHER GOD.** Do not separate yourself from **ME THE FATHER GOD.** Put you and yourself together with **ME**

The Holy Trinity

and we are ONE. We are one entity because **I** speak through you.

Anybody that can think, speak, move or do anything, you are god.

Respect everybody.
Respect your president.
He or she represents **ME THE FATHER GOD.**

Respect your church leader, your religious leader; your King, your Queen, your Prime Minister, your mother, your father and your child. Everybody should respect everybody. Respect one another since you know that **I THE FATHER GOD** lives in everybody.

THE WORD is a costly product. That is **THE FATHER GOD.** That is **SPIRIT.** Even though you may not be able to speak, you are alive. But if finally the **Spirit** leaves you then that means the **WORD** and everything including the **Water** and the **blood** have also left you then you are dead. That is **THE TRINITY** has left you. When the **Spirit** leaves you, then finally the **water** and the **blood** will vanish away and the body will return to dust.

But as long as the **Spirit** still lives in you, it maintains the **Water** and the **blood** and you continue to be a living soul. That is the meaning of **THE HOLY TRINITY.**

THE HOLY TRINITY in Heaven consist of **The Father, The Son** and **The Holy Spirit.**

THE HOLY TRINITY on earth comprises the **Father,** the **Mother** and the **Child.**

THE HOLY TRINITY in the human form, which is in the body, are the **Word,** the **Water** and the **Blood** and all represent **THE FATHER GOD.**

Here we have **God the Father** and **GOD.** Or **THE WORD** and **THE FATHER GOD, THE SPIRIT.**

LET **MY** PEACE AND BLESSING ABIDE WITH THE ENTIRE WORLD, NOW AND FOREVER MORE. *AMEN!*

THANK YOU FATHER!
THANK YOU FATHER!

THANK YOU FATHER! P E A C E - O!

Princess Mfon Etteh offers Prayers of thanks to **THE FATHER GOD.**

*Let thanks and praises be given to **THE FATHER GOD** in the name of Our Lord Jesus Christ. Amen!*
*Let thanks and praises be given to **THE FATHER GOD** in the blood of Our Lord Jesus Christ. Amen!*
*Let thanks and praises be given to **THE FATHER GOD** even now and forever more. Amen!*
*Holy! Holy! Holy! Most loving and EVERLASTING **FATHER GOD,** we give You thanks for this wonderful day that is **THE HOLY TRINITY** Celebration day that you used to superimpose on the negative celebration of this Fourteenth February that the negative spirit confused the whole world with. Thank **YOU FATHER GOD ALMIGHTY, THE DIVINE SPIRIT** of truth that **YOU** have used this Lecture Revelation of today to educate the*

whole world of the error they are committing in celebrating "Valentine Day". Thank You **FATHER GOD ALMIGHTY** *that you have livened up and upgraded the spirits of your positive children so that they would have the awareness of the information of this Lecture Revelation of today, so that they would know themselves and correct their ways. Thank* **YOU PAPA FATHER GOD ALMIGHTY** *that* **YOU** *have come by* **THYSELF** *to your world to put things in order and so make this world a better place.* **Thank FATHER** *that* **YOU** *made it possible for us to partake and witness this wonderful Lecture Revelation and the blessings you bestowed upon us all your positive children all over the world. THANK* **YOU FATHER GOD ALMIGHTY** *for you have made everything perfectly well in the whole world and all is well with us all, even now and forever more. Amen!*

Let thanks and praises be given to **THEE FATHER GOD** *in the name of Our Lord Jesus Christ. Amen!*

The Holy Trinity

Let thanks and praises be given to **THEE FATHER GOD** in the blood of Our Lord Jesus Christ. Amen!

Let thanks and praises be given to **THEE FATHER GOD ALMIGHTY** now and forever more. Amen!

THANK YOU FATHER!

HRM Queen Disem Solomon David **ETE** offers Prayer of thanks to **THE FATHER GOD**

Let thanks and praises be given to **THE FATHER GOD** in the name of Our Lord Jesus Christ. Amen!

Let thanks and praises be given **THE FATHER GOD** in the blood of Our Lord Jesus Christ. Amen!

Let thanks and praises be given to **THE FATHER GOD LEADER OLUMBA OLUMBA OBU**, now and forever more. Amen!

Holy! Holy! Holy!

We thank **YOU** for the Lecture Revelation of today.

We Thank **YOU FATHER GOD THE CREATOR OF THE UNIVERSE** that

The Holy Trinity

YOU have come by **THYSELF** on this Christ day to bring this Lecture Revelation for all **THY** creations. We thank you **FATHER GOD** that through this Lecture Revelation all is perfectly well with the entire mankind who are your physical representatives in **The Trinity** of the **Spirit (Word)** the **Blood** and the **Water.** We thank **YOU FATHER** as **The Trinity** in Heaven, **Father, Son** and the **Holy Spirit** and the **Trinity** on earth, the **father, mother** and the **child** and the **Trinity** in man that you have manifested in as the house to represent **THEE** and glorify **THEE** physically. We thank **YOU FATHER** that the **TRINITY** manifests all good things for all **THY** positive children, even now and forever more. Amen!

    Let thanks and praises be given to **THE FATHER GOD** in the name of Our Lord Jesus Christ. Amen!

    Let thanks and praises be given to **THE FATHER GOD** in the blood of Our Lord Jesus Christ. Amen!

Let thanks and praises be given to The Super Wisdom, the ONE who has come to dispose all negativism. And through this you have superimposed **THE TRINITY GOD** *Celebration on the negativism of 'Valentine Celebration.' And all is perfectly well! And* **YOU** *will continue to reign supreme for eternity, now and forever more. Amen!*

THANK YOU FATHER

Chapter Two

THE FATHER GOD ALMIGHTY, GOD AND GOD THE FATHER

The Holy Trinity

FATHER'S TALK
(GOD PRESENT)

Date: OH/AB/OG (The eighth day of the twelve month of the year two thousand and seven)

In the name of Our Lord Jesus the Christ, In the blood of Our Lord Jesus the Christ, Now and forever, more, *Amien*

THE FATHER GOD ALMIGHTY, GOD AND GOD THE FATHER

It pleases **ME THE FATHER GOD THE CREATOR OF THE UNIVERSE** to open the Spiritual Library once again to reveal some of the hidden treasures as the hidden **UNDERSTANDING** and **WISDOM** for the edification of all children of **GOD** here on this earth.

A: **INTRODUCTION**

From all indications, human beings want to know certain things because in the beginning **I** created man here on earth to study. Here is the school ground as the universe of study, a place of learning where everyone has the opportunity to improve and take evolution to the next life. Due to this, there is a lot of confusion in this world because of the many crafts that people have left behind as condemned ideas. When you improve away from certain things, those things become redundant and unused. This means that they have become waste products and that is why it appears as though the world has become a dumping ground. However, **I AM** now going to sanitize this world and make it a **PERFECT** place to live.

It is only those who worship **THE FATHER GOD** in spirit and in truth that would inherit this world when the

The Holy Trinity

world becomes **PERFECT** after **I** have made everything new. **I** know that so many humankinds no more believe that the world would be **GOOD** and that is why they join the evil side to do whatever that they like. Some people know the truth that when you practice evil, you will pay for it but because the world is full of evil, they decide to join the area that many people have joined.

I AM giving this Lecture Revelation so that you will know the difference between **POSITIVE** and negative. **I AM** revealing **MYSELF** in different ways. **I AM THE FATHER GOD THE CREATOR OF THE UNIVERSE** and at the same time **I AM GOD** and at the same time **I AM GOD THE FATHER**. **I AM** going to reveal the meaning of the **PHENOMENON** of the **TRINITY** and the **TRINITY** in action but **I AM THE ONE** and **ONLY ONE**. If you read many of **THE FATHER'S TALK**, you would know whom **THE FATHER GOD**

The Holy Trinity

is. **HE IS THE SPIRIT** and through **THIS SPIRIT** everything becomes manifest. **HE, THE SPIRIT**, owns **THE WORD** and **THE WORD** owns every physical manifestation. There is no two ways about it. **THE TRUTH** remains the **TRUTH** and it is clear. It is not something that needs repetition however; it would take you to the point in simplicity. There must be simplicity in training and simplicity in understanding and simplicity in putting this **WORD** together for you to understand what **THE FATHER GOD** is because **THE FATHER GOD IS EVERYTHING**.

Do not exclude **THE FATHER GOD** because if you exclude **ME, THE FATHER GOD** in anything that you do, that thing ceases to exist and that is it. The introduction part of this Lecture Revelation is to enable you to open your mind and know that **THE FATHER GOD** exist but if you do not believe that **GOD** exist then you believe that **GOOD** exist. There is no one on this earth as far as humans

The Holy Trinity

are concerned that do not know the meaning of **GOOD** and bad. **I** purposely created that as **POSITIVE** and negative so that all could singularly differentiate the **POSITIVE** and because of that difference, all can also know every bad thing as negative. And from this, you have your human freewill to choose the side that you want be acting with in your life.

If you choose the bad side knowing that, it is bad then the bad energy of negativism will deal with you. Equally, if you choose the **GOOD** side as everyone knows a **GOOD** thing and what it is to be **GOOD** and likes **GOOD** things then the **GOOD** energy of **POSITIVISM** will deal with you. When **MY** energy is dealing with you, the manifestation will be exactly what you will see. The manifestation of **GOOD** will always bring **GOOD** things such as a **GOOD** life, **GOOD** future and everything **GOOD**. You can imagine how it can be if the **TOTALITY** of **ALL GOOD** plays a part

The Holy Trinity

in support of you. And you can also imagine how it can be if the totality of all bad is in attendance with you and this is why you must use your freewill to choose. Since **I AM LOVE**, **I** created man with the freewill to operate because everything done from ones freewill is well done. **I** do not like to force the situation even though **I** can force everybody in this world to do exactly what **I** want in a second because **I** live in everyone and everything and control all things. However, forcing things does not give **ME** glory because it means that **I AM** literally doing that job. That is why **I** give man freewill in operation so that it looks 'some what' as though you are a separate body.

You know that when you cook food for someone that is very hungry, they will enjoy it more than the one that they cook by themselves. When you give someone honour and glory they enjoy it more than the one that they give to themselves but despite this the glory and honour belongs to whoever that deserves it. The introduction of this Lecture Revelation is to enable you to be in spirit and open your mind as a lover of **GOOD** things because what you are going to hear today is about **GOOD** things and the **POSITIVE** side of **THE FATHER GOD**.

THE POSITIVE PHENOMENA'S as **THE EXISTENCE** and the only **THING** that controls everything is **THE FATHER GOD, GOD,** and **GOD THE FATHER**. You will know about the impact and the meaning of **OOO** as **GOD THE FATHER, GOD** and also **THE FATHER GOD** in either order that form the **SUPREME OOO** that supersedes all powers in heaven and on earth. **MY COMPLETION IN TOTALITY** is **OOO**. **O** in heaven, **O** in the soul and **O** here on earth. **I** have said before that, **I THE FATHER GOD THE CREATOR OF THE UNIVERSE** lives in three dimensions which are everywhere, here and there as **THE THREE RING CIRCLES,(THE**

The Holy Trinity

TOTALITY OF ALL INCLUDED). **HE IS THE FATHER** lives **EVERYWHERE**, **HERE** and **THERE**. You know the meaning of everywhere, you know the meaning of here and you also know the meaning of there. No matter the language of interpretation, everywhere, here and there is understandable. And that is the meaning of **OOO**.

B: **THE FATHER GOD ALMIGHTY**

What is the meaning of **THE ALMIGHTY FATHER GOD**? It means **THE FATHER** that made **GOD**. All souls, all spirits, all angles, all unseen, all seen, all untouchable, all touchable, all unheard, and all heard and all things put together are produced by **HE IS THE FATHER**, **THE ALMIGHTY FATHER GOD**. In this Lecture Revelation, **I** will explain things so that man would not be confused again. Do not think that this Lecture Revelation came from a human being and do not equalise this

The Holy Trinity

Lecture Revelation, **THE FATHER'S TALK (GOD PRESENT)** to be like any seminar that you may receive in the world or going to church to receive preaching or going to a secret society to learn. **I** have travelled a long journey to the earth today to make possible **THE FATHER'S TALK (GOD PRESENT)** which is the direct **WORD** from **ME THE FATHER GOD THE CREATOR OF THE UNIVERSE**. In those days when **I** used to talk through prophets, **I** used to pass through angels, as **I** did not have direct access to man because of man's situation. However, since **I** came as **GOD** the son to come and die on earth as **I** promised to salvage mankind through the shedding of **MY HOLY** blood and flesh, **I** can talk directly to man. And through this, **I** have redeemed man and now that **I** have redeemed man, **I** have where to live again.

Senior Christ Servant, HRM King Solomon David Jesse **ETE** is the

The Holy Trinity

original Abel however, **I** could not talk through him today if not for Our Lord Jesus Christ shedding his blood. It is not because he is very **GOOD** or that he is holy but it is because his **FATHER** has died for him and sanctified him therefore, **I** speak through Him as a servant of **GOD**. This is his mission and the reason for his creation. He is a **DESIGNER TOOL** of creation as the **MEMORY** of **GOD**, the earmarked **HOLY GHOST** as the first ghost in the old scenario as Abel, the first person that died.

He who dies first also resurrects first. And the first man that caused the first death was his senior brother Cain and he remains as the everlasting evil as the king in hell. There is nothing to do about negativism. You can only prison negativism. The supreme vampire, death, it self as Satan is in the hell fire. He has no remedy and there is nothing he can do. If you do not prison bad, you cannot get **GOOD** to work. If you do not condemn your

The Holy Trinity

bad attitude then you cannot change to **GOOD**. If you cannot forget about evil, you cannot leave evil. There is no two ways about it; evil is in prison in the hell fire.

The first Holy Ghost is the soul of Abel and his **FATHER** died to resurrect him and that is why the spirit of Abel has come back on earth as the **TALKING, TALKING** and that is what you are hearing today. There is no two ways about it! Whether you believe it or not the **TRUTH** remains for eternity as the **TRUTH**. **I THE FATHER GOD THE CREATOR OF THE UNIVERSE** is using **SUPREME LOVE, SUPREME HUMILITY, SUPREME PEACE**, and **SUPREME ONENESS** to bring this notice back on earth so that the divine children of **GOD** should not perish because of ignorance from not studying and understanding.

If you follow **FATHER'S TALK (GOD PRESENT)** Lecture Revelations gradually as the case study of the

The Holy Trinity

higher student in the School of the Higher Self Brotherhood Mastership, then you will help your soul out of your ignorant situation. The wide angle of **ME** is **WISDOM** and through the **WISDOM** of **GOD**, you will become closer to **GOD**. **THE ALMIGHTY FATHER GOD** means the spirit that created everything. Without **HIM**, there is nothing, not even **THE SPOKEN WORD**. Where did **THE WORD** come from and who made the **WORD** to be **ALL** and **ALL**? Before **THE WORD** hutched, there is something that engineered **THE WORD** which is **THE SUPREME THOUGHT**. **I** have given a Lecture Revelation titled, ***THE SUPREME SILENT THOUGHT***.

You have to understand that one thing leads to the other. **THE SUPREME FATHER GOD HE IS THE SPIRIT** is the ark of everything of everything. That is where all human beings and all creations came from. And for this reason, you must obey and acknowledge this **HE IS THE**

FATHER and **HE IS THE SPIRIT** and if you do this, you will not have any problem again. When you acknowledge **THIS SPIRIT, HE IS THE FATHER GOD**, adore **HIM**, know **HIM** and worship **HIM** then all is well with you in the spirit, the soul and the truth. The short introduction for this Lecture Revelation is simple. It is not something to talk about for long periods. **THE PHENOMENON** which is **THE FATHER GOD** is **THE EXISTENCE** from which everything else came out and you may call it a **SPIRIT, SOUL** or **PHYSICAL** but that is **THE RIGHTFUL OWNER** and the head of **BROTHERHOOD**. That is Brotherhood in spirit, in the soul and in the physical truth.

C: **GOD ALMIGHTY**

We have now entered into the second **O, GOD ALMIGHTY**. In spirit, **I** have defined the letter '**G**' for many things and one day; **I** will give a Lecture Revelation about letter '**G**'

The Holy Trinity

just as **I** revealed letter '**W**' as the **WIDE ANGLE** of **GOD** - **WISDOM**. **G** means general. **G** means **GOVERNMENT**, to **GOVERN** which is power. **G** also means **GO** and **GOD** which means spirit, as the actor, introduction and the power of being. To say **GO** is like to say **LET** but **GO** exist before **LET**. The middle **O** is the power of **LET** which is the energy of **WORD** as the amplifier of **GEN**, **THE SPOKEN WORD** and it means that **GO** comes before **LET**.

In the physical world, you will say **LET GO** or **LET ME BE** but in spirit, **GO** is first and that is **THE SPIRIT ITSELF**, '**G**' and that is the command word, the energy of generality, government and that is why **I** call it **GOD** and **GOOD**. **GOD ALMIGHTY** is **THE SPOKEN WORD** and that is the way in which **I** came as the son of **GOD**. Every human being is God. **GOD** means the **SPOKEN WORD** as the energy of **THE FATHER GOD** is **THE WORD**. The soul of **THE FATHER GOD** is the **WORD** and that

The Holy Trinity

WORD means **GOD ALMIGHTY** and when this **WORD** becomes flesh that is what **I** shall reveal towards the end making three **O**'s as **OOO** in total. The first **O** is **THE FATHER GOD**, **THE ONE** that made **GOD**, and **THE ONE** that made the **WORD** as **THE OWNER OF THE WORD** and **THE FATHER** of **THE WORD** as the energy that brought the **WORD** into existence. **THE FATHER GOD** means **THE FATHER** of **GOD** but since there is no separation and **WE** are **ONE** that is, why **I** say **FATHER GOD**. However if you want to separate then **IT** is **THE FATHER** of **GOD** but who is **THE FATHER GOD**, **HE** is **GOD HIMSELF**. For this reason, **THE SPOKEN WORD** is **GOD ALMIGHTY** and that is the maker of heaven and earth. **GOD ALMIGHTY** is the manifestation of **THE FATHER** in reality from **REAL** to **REALSO** and from **REALSO** to **AMISO**. If you check **THE FATHER'S TALK**, you will know that **THE ALMIGHTY FATHER GOD** has created **GOD ALMIGHTY** to be **HIS**

machinery as the servant. And through **THE ALMIGHTY FATHER GOD, GOD ALMIGHTY** is manifesting every creation on earth and that is the second **O, GO**. What does **GO** do? That is the ergo, as the force, the energy that brings things into existence and makes things happen as **GO**. And in-between **GO, LET** is standing by to manifest the command and that is the energy of **THE SPOKEN WORD**. Everything has an internal and an external drive as a result of input and output. And everything has an external outfit and that is why there is **GO** and **LET**. **GO** is the owner of **LET** and **LET** is the owner of manifestation as **THE SPOKEN WORD**.

D: **GOD THE FATHER**

We have now arrived at the third **O**, which is **GOD THE FATHER**. The first **O** is **THE FATHER GOD**, the second **O** is **GOD ALMIGHTY** and this is **GOD THE FATHER** as **ALPHA** and

The Holy Trinity

OMEGA. This is the first manifestation house of the **SPOKEN WORD** as Adam. And that is the son of man because man is **GOD HIMSELF**. This is **THE KINGS** of **KINGS** and **THE LORD** of **LORDS** as the **OWNER** of everything and the caretaker of the whole universe therefore **THE THREE** are **ONE PHENOMENON**. If you worship any of **THEM**, you worship each of **THEM**. Any of **THEM** is any of **THEM** as **THEY** are **ALL ONE**. There is no way that you would worship **GOD ALMIGHTY** and **THE FATHER GOD** would query why you worship **GOD ALMIGHTY**. And there is no way that if you give glory and respect to **GOD THE FATHER** that **GOD ALMIGHTY** or **THE FATHER GOD** will become annoyed because it is **ONE SPIRIT** that has manifested into these three capacities. Without **THE ALMIGHTY FATHER GOD**, there will not be **GOD ALMIGHTY** as the spirit, **THE SPOKEN WORD** and without **THE SPOKEN WORD**, there will not be anything like **GOD THE FATHER** which a human being as the first man on earth who was Adam. You can now understand that through **THE ALMIGHTY FATHER GOD, THE WORD** manifests. And **THE WORD** manifests the creation and man and lives inside man therefore Adam is the **GOD THE FATHER** in human form and everybody on earth must worship the divined Adam. In the beginning, Adam made a mistake because he was a baby. **I** told him that he should not touch but he touched.

    I AM going to give another Lecture Revelation titled '*A BABY SHOULD NOT TOUCH AND SHOULD NOT SPEAK; A BABY SHOULD LOOK AND LISTEN*'. When Adam was a baby in nature, he was not supposed to touch and speak. He was supposed to be silent and learn until he grew and then he could act, but when he did not do that because of the enemy (the negative self that deceived him) that is when the problem started. You can learn more about this in many of

The Holy Trinity

the Lecture Revelations that **I** have given so we are not going back to that again.

Today, we are straitening things so that during **THE FATHER'S** physical birthday, all children of **GOD** should be happy, rejoice and worship **THE FATHER GOD** with a free mind without doubt and fear. Some people ask you why you worship a human being and believe in **OLUMBA OLUMBA OBU** and this and that and others ask why you believe in **OUR LORD JESUS CHRIST** and so on and so forth. All these questions amount to lack of understanding and ignorance which has caused people to perish.

Who is **OUR LORD JESUS CHRIST**? Who are you, your person? Don't you know that you are **OUR LORD JESUS CHRIST**? Every human being on earth is the same person. And you are going to hear about this later. **THE ALMIGHTY FATHER GOD, GOD ALMIGHTY** and **GOD THE**

The Holy Trinity

FATHER, **ALPHA** and **OMEGA**, the beginning and the ever forwarding is the **ONE** that the **SPIRIT** lives in, in the three capacities. In man, there is a **SPIRIT**, in man, there is **THE WORD**, in man there is **THE BODY** therefore in man the trinity manifest as blood, water and spirit. This why **THE FATHER GOD** lives in man and **THE WORD** of **GOD** also lives in man and man is the tabernacle of **GOD** here on earth. And for this reason, man should respect himself. **I AM** going to give a Lecture Revelation titled '***MAN IS THE MOST RESPECTABLE PHENOMENON***' so that you will know that **I AM** not joking anymore.

E: **ALL HUMANS ARE ONE**

We have come to the understanding that every human being is Adam and that is the reason that all humans are one. If you say to someone that you are the father, it means that you are also the father.

The Holy Trinity

Do you not see that your father gave birth to you and you also gave birth to someone and that person then calls you his or her father? And your son who calls you father will also have a child and that child will call him father therefore in a situation like this, do you not know that there are no two people on earth?

Are you as stupid and ignorant as not to realise this knowledge? This why **LOVE** is the only answer and that is why if you do not **LOVE** yourself then you destroy yourself. That is why if you hate anyone you hate yourself and that is why it is only evil that can hate because if you hate you are a baby in nature with no understanding and that means that you are stupid. If you are wicked to someone, you are being wicked to yourself and that is why you should not go near a wicked person or condone them for any reason. **LOVE** everyone but have no business with anyone that **I** reveal to you as a wicked person. Anyone that has evil spirit is wicked and has wicked intentions and that is why you should not have any association with that person because he or she has already perished. What do you do with faeces as a perished product? You throw it away because it is waste.

I do not have to have patience for waste things and do not have to waste time for waste things because in a very short time in this world, you will see that all wicked people are going to destroy themselves if they do not change now and take a personal evolution by confessing and changing all their negative ways. It is not too late because as long as you are alive anything can happen. Don't be happy because **THE FATHER** is all and all and therefore you hide under that and practise evil and say that **THE FATHER** has something to do with evil things. **I** have finally come to reveal all these things so that **I** will separate **POSITIVE** from negative because for generations upon generations negative has been spoiling **POSITIVE**. Now **THE LIGHT**

is shining by **ITSELF**. It is self chargeable batteries and you do not need to connect to anyone or anything. **I** have an inbuilt **HOLY SPIRIT** as a **STAR** in you that will if you give **ME** the opportunity by practicing **LOVE**. You do not need anyone or anything to make you shine.

You should shine in **THE FATHER GOD**. All human beings are one person, just one single person but **I** have synchronised, duplicated and copied it many times over. Just as if you make one master copy of a document for printing but you can use the master to produce millions of copies. **I** used the original template and produce many duplicates. Is that the bad thing that **I** have done through **LOVE** as the '***Only singular that has become plural***'? Have you read this **FATHER'S TALK**? When you read it, you will know that, it is through **LOVE** that **I** made everything exist including man. Why should man that **I** create in **MY** own image and

The Holy Trinity

likeness come back to fight **GOD**. Why do you kick against the truth and be annoyed about **THE FATHER'S TALK**, (**GOD PRESENT**) or about HRM King Solomon or are annoyed about anybody? Some people ask such questions as who is Christ. Who is Mohamed or who is Isaac and who is Ishmael? They are all Abraham. Where did Isaac come from? He came from Abraham and so did Ishmael, therefore Jesus Christ and Mohamed are one. Are they not from one **GOD** and one **FATHER**? Are Adam and Eve not from one **FATHER**? What is the difference?

Show **ME** where the Black man and the White man came from. Who are the mother and father of Black man and White man? If you refuse to accept this truth and **LOVE** everyone then that thing that you hate and condemn and say is not good will be - - - unless that thing is negative.

You should not attach yourself to negativism or wicked people rather attach yourself to any good person or any good thing. Do not attach yourself to someone because he or she is Black or White as the colour of the person does not determine a good or a bad person. Also, a person from Africa or from a European country does not determine whether that person is good or bad.

It is the same air that you breathe here that you will breathe anywhere else. However if you pollute the air in England then you will get good air in Africa. That is what it is. If you have good water, here you can have that water everywhere and that is what it is. **LOVE** means generality and that is the meaning of **GOD**. And as a result, the government is representing **GOD** as **LOVE**. Now you should understand that every human being is one.

People often ask why the life span of man is short. The reason is that when Adam was alone, he lived for nearly one thousand years and almost lived forever was because there were not many duplications of life. However, now that **I** have shared the plural of Adams as one life for everyone, life has shortened. Do not forget that the more you copy something the more the original thing fades away. And that is why sometimes after making a copy and you have a lot more copies to make, you should use one of the copies to make more copies so that you can preserve the original copy. However, those that you copy the second or third time will fade further. If you do not do that then you may need to make another master copy as a template.

Now **I** have made a master copy through the power of **THE HOLY SPIRIT**. A new human being on earth must have the **HOLY SPIRIT** as a **TEMPLATE**. If you do not have the **HOLY SPIRIT**, you cannot be new. The people that are still at the stage of Adam are the people that have many problems and make a lot of mistakes. They do not understand

The Holy Trinity

things because they are still living a primitive life. However, those who came out from the first natural Adam to the Adam of the spirit, the soul which is **CHRIST** as **OUR LORD JESUS THE CHRIST** who is now elevated to **LOVE** and **GOD ALMIGHTY** are without problems. When you are elevated to **GOD** and the **LOVE** of **GOD** then you have taken a new evolution to a new life.

MY only commandment is to **LOVE ONE ANOTHER** and that is the law that your Father Adam, the new Adam gave to you. The second Adam is the parent who came to create a new law for his child. Do you know that **OUR LORD JESUS CHRIST** is not the son? He is only a son to **THE SPIRIT** which created everything which is **THE FATHER GOD** but he is **GOD ALMIGHTY**. If you say that you do not want to worship **OUR LORD JESUS CHRIST** because **HE** is a human being and that he is supposed to be a prophet and not the son of

The Holy Trinity

GOD then do not forget that **HE** is not even the son of **GOD HE** is **GOD HIMSELF**. Have you not heard that the **WORD** became man and lived among men? That is the second Adam. The second Adam is **HIS** soul creator where the first Adam is the physical creator. It is the **WORD**, created by **ME, THE FATHER GOD** that created Adam physically. That is the meaning of the anointed one.

The anointed one is **THE SPOKEN WORD**. Who rules the whole world? When **I** say that **CHRIST** is ruling, do you think that **HE** is going to sit down in a big chair and rule man? The judge, the teacher, a child, an adult, a man, a woman and everyone in all positions are using **THE WORD** therefore who is ruling? Is it not **THE WORD**? And that is **THE CHRIST OF GOD, THE KING OF KINGS** and **THE LORD OF LORDS**. And that is **GOD ALMIGHTY**.

GOD ALMIGHTY'S HOME is **GOD THE FATHER**, the **ALPHA** and

The Holy Trinity

OMEGA. This is the head of all human beings however, these days people, crafty as they are, do not want to respect their Father. When **I** say that if you speak ill about **THE FATHER, I** may forgive you, or if you speak ill about the son you may be forgiven but if you speak ill about the **HOLY SPIRIT** of **TRUTH** you will not be forgiven, what is the meaning of that?

 THE ALMIGHTY FATHER GOD, **GOD** and **GOD THE FATHER**, the **ALPHA** and **OMEGA** is the spirit and the soul that lives in the human body that manifested as the third **O** called **OLUMBA OLUMBA OBU** as the last Adam, the universal shrine. And everybody on earth must accept this. And this why when you hate **OOO**, you hate your soul and life just as when you hate **CHRIST**, you hate your soul and your life. And who is **CHRIST**? Is **HE** not **OOO** and who is **OOO**? It is Adam, **THE FATHER, THE SON** and **THE HOLY SPIRIT** and that is what it is. The spirit lives in the soul and the soul lives in whom? Do

The Holy Trinity

you not think and speak? Do you not have blood and water? And how does that blood be alive? It is through the spirit which generates the blood and the water in you to make you a living soul.

If the **SPIRIT** leaves you then the water becomes cold and melts to the ground and you will go back to the sand because you are no more alive and that means that the owner of the house that warmed the house has gone and that is **ME**, the part of **GOD** in you. When **THE FATHER GOD** becomes man, **HE** becomes **GOD ALMIGHTY** and that is a spirit called **THE SPOKEN WORD**. When **THE FATHER GOD** and **THE SPIRIT OF THE FATHER** becomes man, it manifests through the water, blood and spirit and becomes a human being and that is Emmanuel meaning **GOD** is with man which is **THE SPOKEN WORD**. Adam was the first son of **GOD** as **THE** only begotten son of **THE FATHER** and **HE** is **GOD**. When you say that you are not going

The Holy Trinity

to worship a human being, do you know that from the beginning of time when **I** created Adam and lived in Him, every other creation worshiped him because that is their **GOD**? Your father is your **GOD** and your mother is your **GOD** if you do not know? Even you senior brother is your **GOD**. That is why every creation, including all birds, animals, fishes, all other living creatures and living organisms must worship their Father, Adam, **GOD ALMIGHTY**, the Alpha and Omega.

If you had not known these things, then know it today. This Lecture Revelation should serve as a point of correction to the entire universe so that you will not doubt because people are worshiping **THE FATHER GOD** with elements of doubt. They ask all sorts of questions such as, 'why should I knock my head for a human being'? 'Why should I respect a human being'? Since you refuse to respect your father, do your children respect you? This is why you must respect your Father. Since you do not honour **THE WORD**, does **THE WORD** honour you? As you use **THE WORD** unnecessarily, **THE WORD** is now making a case with you. **THE WORD** would judge everybody on this earth that misuses **THE WORD** because they shall stand for condemnation if they are not able to justify what they used **THE WORD** to do. For this reason, do not toy with **THE SPIRIT**, your thought and **THE WORD** and do not toy with man because these three capacities are very important phenomena's.

F: ALL CREATIONS ARE IN HUMANS

If human beings have the spirit of **GOD** in them, then they are **GOD** but not **GOD ALMIGHTY** because the only **GOD ALMIGHTY** in the human form is Adam. And the second Adam is **OUR LORD JESUS CHRIST** who came to die for mankind and that spirit is **THE HOLY SPIRIT OF TRUTH. I** have restored that office back as the **KING of Kings** and the **LORD of Lords** who is the final Adam, has the physical **OLUMBA OLUMBA OBU**, for eternity. **THE KING of Kings** and **THE LORD of Lords** is a Spirit and also a human being. **GOD** is a SPIRIT but do not equalize a human being with that SPIRIT therefore every human house must respect that SPIRIT that lives in **HIM**. You should now understand and if you do not understand, then you need to fast and pray for understanding, because it is a case of the more you look, the less you see. When you knock **your** head on the ground, for whom do you think that **you** knock **your** head for? Do you think that **you** knock **your** head for a human being like you? This flesh and blood cannot be **GOD ALMIGHTY**. **GOD ALMIGHTY** lives in man and when you kneel down and knock your head you are recognizing that **SPIRIT** that lives in you and around you which is **GOD ALMIGHTY, THE SPOKEN WORD** and that is **THE**

The Holy Trinity

LORD, THE KING of **KINGS** and **THE LORD** of **LORDS** who resides in all human beings. If **HE** resides in **HIM** then **HE** also resides in **YOU**. What is the difference between one man and the other man? Every human being must **LOVE** because every human being is the house of **GOD**. You must **LOVE** each other and understand each other because in every situation there is a head and a head office. And **I** created Adam as the first son of **THE FATHER GOD** and he is the first son of **GOD** because **THE SPOKEN WORD** first resided in Adam.

This house of Adam has become the reason that you cannot change this arrangement. And that is why **I** came as **THE SPOKEN WORD** to die, destroy negativism and renovate the temple of **GOD**, the universal shrine as the first begotten son and the first son of man. This is how **GOD** has come down on earth as the physical **OLUMBA OLUMBA OBU**. The spiritual **OLUMBA OLUMBA OBU** is **THE SPIRIT** as **THE SPIRIT OF**

The Holy Trinity

TRUTH. The physical **ONE** is **THE FATHER** of all humans called **GOD THE FATHER ALMIGHTY**, the Alpha and Omega. In spirit, **HE** is **GOD ALMIGHTY** but physically here on earth, **HE** is **THE KING of Kings** and **THE LORD of Lords** because the spirit as **THE SPOKEN WORD** is **THE KING OF KINGS AND THE LORD OF LORDS**. The spirit of **THE SPOKEN WORD** that is dwelling in **HIM** as **THE KING OF KINGS** and **THE LORD OF LORDS** is your **FATHER**. And anybody that knocks his or her head and believes this is blessed.

All creations are in humans hence there is human fish, human bird and human animal. Why should **I** call them human fish, human bird, and human animal? It is because all these creations that **I** have created before man are taking evolution to develop into human beings. A human being is the centre of development capacity because human being is the world of another spiritual space. When you see people walking on the street, do you know what lives in them and whom they represent and what they stand for? A human being is a house, just as you may see different buildings but you do not know what is in them. You cannot even know what is in another room in your house where someone else lives and you will not know what they do there and what they keep in the room? And that is why you must humble yourself to learn.

This is the school of the higher self so that when you grow you will reach the stage of higher consciousness so that you do not make so many mistakes again. You will become an arranged person in the way you talk, the way you look and what you think will all be re- arranged because now you will understand a certain way of life. When you do not go to school and you do not travel to many places you cannot understand certain things however, the more exposure you have about certain things, the more you understand what is going on and the more self awareness that you will have. If you are humble today and listen to these Lecture Revelations then you will learn a lot of things. Whatever it may cost you, you have to listen to as many of the different Lecture Revelations from **THE FATHER'S TALK (GOD PRESENT)** as you can. **I** have assigned seventy two million records as Lecture Revelations for release to this earth and it does not really mater about the time table.

All human beings are one with other creations because some of the humans that you see are not actual human beings. They are taking the form of a human house but something else is living inside of them. That is why **I** said that all creations are inside human beings. When you see, people behave, as animals do not say that they act as animals because they are actually real animals. Some people are behaving as dogs. When you watch people's characters and their

The Holy Trinity

way of life, you will see so many animals acting in them. You will also see **GOD** acting through man. A man that **GOD** is acting through is very intelligent. First of all, you will see **PEACE, HUMILITY, PATIENCE, MERCY, KINDNESS** and **LOVE** and at least you will see the five major fruits and five major stars in that person as **MERCY, PEACE, LOVE, KINDNESS** and **RIGHTEOUSNESS** which signify that **GOD** dwells in that person and he or she is a human **GOD** as the house of **GOD**. Such a person is not a human fish, a human bird, or human animal.

If you see any human being that speaks and behaves in an animalistic manner by fighting, quarrelling and generally being wicked then they are animals. Sometimes physically, they behave very well but in spirit, they are wicked people. They go about turning themselves into animals to wicked people. No human God can turn themselves into an animal to bewitch people. Why and how should

The Holy Trinity

people turn themselves into owls or into fishes to go into the water and all other types of animals to do all sorts of things? It is because, that is their nature. You can only go back to your nature, you cannot go back to what you are not and that is why you should not say that it is witchcraft. The reason that **I** say that there is nothing like witchcraft or anything like a secret society or anything is because **I** know that originally, **I** do not create those things, which means that those things are what they are because they are created by you-human being.

    I created everything for a reason of positives ideas, but since they have taken an evolution to be wicked, they have become waste products and they cannot go higher than that. Every positive creation that develops to become a man would **LOVE ONE ANOTHER**, living **PEACEFULLY** as a child of **GOD**. There are so many children of **GOD** in human fish, human bird and human animal and there is so much evil corruption in human Gods. There are human Gods that have turned to be evil because if you are created as a proper man and you are not positive then you join serpent and vampires and practice all sorts of wickedness. By so doing you take a backward evolution by reducing your glory to that of a human animal, bird and fish. Sometimes you end up joining witchcraft purposely or in the name of looking for money or power then you start to practice wickedness.

Imagine a child of **GOD** that goes to look for money and when you go they say that you should offer your child or your mother and you sign for it instead of rebuking such a condition and disgracing it. Even if you might die, it is better to die for **GOOD** than to die for evil or even live for evil. To die for **GOOD** is better than to live for evil because you are already dead.

All creations are in human forms and all humans are in different creations but positive human **GOD** triumphant over all things because they are the representatives of **GOD THE FATHER** on earth.

G: **HUMANKIND AND THE FATHER GOD**

Today is a very **GOOD** day due to this Lecture Revelation which has come in advance for **THE FATHER'S** birthday. When we talk about **THE FATHER'S** birth, it is not the birthday of **THE FATHER GOD** nor is it the birthday of **GOD OF ALMIGHTY**; it is the birthday of **GOD THE FATHER**. When you call someone **FATHER**, there is one that is **THE FATHER** and that is the **ONE** you know as **OOO** physically, the Alpha and Omega who is originally the physical house of Adam and now the physical **OLUMBA OLUMBA OBU**. Every creation must **POSITIVELY** interlink and accept this and that is why **I** say that there is no division again in **THE FATHER GOD** since **I** have decided to bring

The Holy Trinity

everybody together and make **PEACE** in the whole world through **UNDERSTANDING** in the Name and Blood of Our Lord Jesus Christ. Misunderstanding brings problems, scattering, quarrelling, fighting and killing through the spirit of negative people. However, through the **LOVE** of **GOD**, **I** have poured the **HOLY SPIRIT** to all creations and all human beings. You will see that in a very short time all Christians will live together with Muslims without any problems.

All Muslims will live together with Christians without problems and the western world would live together with Africans without problems and Africans and the Asia's and the western world will all live well. Indeed all human beings must live well.

If you bypass **ME** to hate and destroy or practice wickedness of any kind, **I** will ensure that you immediately destroy yourself first so that you can taste what you have portioned for another person. **I** have

The Holy Trinity

sent millions of angels and **I AM** in those angels therefore you cannot bribe them. In a very short time, the juju that you are worshiping will hold your neck and ask you why you worship it. And in a very short time, the talisman that you buy will hold your neck and ask you why you sacrifice for it.

You will see that all the evil that you practice will turn against you because there is no evil master again and that means no evil energy anymore. One day **I** will cease all the energy of negativism and you will see that when you go back to those things you will see what will happen to you. **I AM** only waiting to make sure that the information goes around then **I** will do **MY** will on earth.

Nobody should be afraid of anything. You should only be afraid if you do not have **LOVE** then be afraid of evil but if you are **POSITIVE**, do not be afraid because you stand on

The Holy Trinity

the rock that will never fail. **THE ALMIGHTY FATHER GOD** is taking care of **GOD** and **GOD** is taking care of **GOD THE FATHER**, the Alpha and Omega. The Alpha and Omega covers all his children and all his other selves. Every human being on earth came from one SUPREME FATHER and MOTHER, therefore, **I THE FATHER GOD THE CREATOR OF THE UNIVERSE** has covered you and that is the meaning of this Lecture Revelation.

CONCLUSION A: **STOP DOUBTING GOD**.

Through this Lecture Revelation, you should stop doubting **GOD**. Give this Lecture Revelation to anyone that says that you are worshiping man as **GOD ALMIGHTY** and **GOD THE FATHER**. You are to respect man as your father and mother as you respect and **LOVE** your self then respect yourself as the house of **GOD**. And by respecting and **LOVING** each other, you are worshiping **GOD** in **SPIRIT** and in **TRUTH** and that is the meaning of worshiping **GOD** in spirit and in **TRUTH**. What is the truth? **GOD THE FATHER** is the house of **GOD ALMIGHTY**. And **THE FATHER GOD** manifests through **GOD ALMIGHTY** therefore with this arrangement, what is the centre, the tabernacle or the church of **GOD**? When you talk about a house of **GOD** and the tabernacle of **GOD**, it all ends in the human self and the body when a human being is alive. That is why when you see man, you have seen **GOD** and you have seen **THE FATHER GOD** and that is what it is. We are children of **THE FATHER GOD** and the reason being is we are plenty. You cannot **FATHER** when you are plenty. **THE FATHER** means one thing and a son means one single male and children of **GOD** means plural of humans both men and women. For this reason, we are fathers in the sons as the servants of **GOD**. As a result, **GOD** is manifesting

The Holy Trinity

HIMSELF through us and that makes us **GOD'S** because we are the house of **GOD**. From today, **THE FATHER'S** will have manifested in man and you must stop doubting **GOD** because by doubting yourself, you inevitably doubt **GOD**. When you believe in yourself, you believe **GOD**.

CONCLUSION B: YOU ARE THE HOUSE OF GOD AS THE POSITIVE THINKER

What is the meaning of **GOD**? The meaning of **GOD** is in two capacities. **GOD** is **THE WORD**. And where did **THE FATHER** engineer **HIS** son? It is through **THOUGHT, THE SUPREME THOUGHT** because **POSITIVE THINKING** brings a **POSITIVE WORD** which is **GOD** and negative thought brings a negative word which is evil and that is Satan. You are the house of the **POSITIVE THOUGHT** if you are **POSITIVE** and **THINK POSITIVELY** then you are a house for **GOD** and as you are housing

The Holy Trinity

GOD, THE FATHER and the Son will live in you and will manifest their glory in you and you will receive wonderful blessings. If people call, oh **FATHER, FATHER**, they will see **HIM** in you! And oh, Son, Son they will see **HIM** in you and then you will receive all amounts of '*kudi kudi*' blessings, (fringe benefits). If you are serving a shrine as a spirit, the spirit will bring people and those people will bring food and glory. If you give the glory to that spirit then you can take the food. All the money and all the things that people bring as sacrifice would be eaten by you because all that is required by the shrine, as the spirit, is the recognition. All that **I** want as **THE FATHER GOD** is **RECOGNITION**. And when you understand this and have **LOVE** and have **PEACE** and have **PATIENCE** and have **KINDNESS** and have **ONENESS** then all is well with **ME** and you but when you practice evil, wickedness, hate one another have strife, anger and are jealous then you

The Holy Trinity

are in trouble because **I** will desert you. However, when you **LOVE, THINK WELL, SPEAK WELL**, and **DO WELL**, **I** will never leave you comfortless. **I** will prove to you that **I AM THE SPIRIT COMFORTER**.

CONCLUSION C: **DIVINE YOUR MIND AND HEART FOR GOD**

Now that you have read and heard this Lecture revelation and **I** have given you directives through **THE MANUAL OF LIFE, INVESTMENT WITH GOD**, and all **THE FATHER'S TALK** that you read and study, then **I** will develop you and you will become a changed personality. And who would be that **PERSONALITY**; it is **THE FATHER GOD** in you. You should **DIVINE YOUR HEART WELL** through this Lecture Revelation so that you will **THINK WELL, SPEAK WELL** and **DO WELL**. No matter the amount of evil that lives in you, since you accept **THE FATHER GOD**, **I** will wash you clean and sanitize you

The Holy Trinity

because **I AM** the force of energy. When **I** enter you through your mind because you accept, then **I** will clean the environment and send all rubbish away then the house becomes a **POSITIVE** house of **GOD**. From then you **THINK POSITIVE, SPEAK POSITIVE** and **DO POSITIVE**. From today, **DIVINE** your mind by accepting **THE TRUTH** and accepting **AFTER THOSE DAYS SAYS THE LORD MOST HIGH** through which, **I** promised that **I** would be **TALKING, TALKING**. This is what **I** was looking for. Why should **I** be coming to the world all the time? **I** came to the world to establish **MYSELF** and now **I AM** the establishment.

    I have given the **EVERLASTING GOSPEL** and now is the **TESTIMONY OF EVERLASTING GOSPEL** which is **THE FATHER'S TALK (GOD PRESENT)**. It is for the student of the higher self in the School of the Higher Self, **BROTHERHOOD MASTERSHIP**. You must reach the stage of **MASTERSHIP** because there

The Holy Trinity

are levels of graduation from **UNDERSTANDING THE FATHER GOD** and **UNDERSTANDING** yourself. When you know yourself, you shall know all things then as a result of that, you will **THINK WELL**, **SPEAK WELL** and **DO WELL** then the world will change for **GOOD**. It is not magic. The only magic is that when you continue to destroy the world then you will inevitably destroy yourself. It is not **THE FATHER** that will destroy you; it is you who will destroy yourself because what you sow is what you will reap.

Divine your heart and your mind for **GOD** to live in you and manage your environment. When the **HOLY SPIRIT** lives you because you are **PEACEFUL**, because you **LOVE**, because you are **PATIENT**, because you are **HUMBLE**, because you are have **MERCY** then the **POSITIVE** SPIRIT will send away all evil and Satan cannot live in you again because she has no glory.

You see, in this world, people do not like to publish **GOOD** news because they say that there is no excitement. People are excited about negativism and because of that, they hide all the **POSITIVE** news but in the kingdom of **GOD**, excitement is for **POSITIVE** news such as someone has given birth, or someone has passed their exams and so forth. Why do you not publicise such news? The more you emphasis negative news, the more you progress and promote negativism.

From today, the **POSITIVE, POSITIVE, POSITIVE** has come to reign in your house. When you stand with **THE FATHER GOD** to desert evil and condemn all manners of evil in your heart then you will see a new life, you will have **GOOD** health and have **GOOD** dreams and **I** will send away all negativisms from you. If you know that anyone around you is negative, do not have anything to do with that person. Try all possible means to segregate yourself away

The Holy Trinity

from evil. This is not because you do not **LOVE** them but if you say that **THE FATHER GOD** is **LOVE** and you go and mingle with drunkards, witches and wizards and all manners of people involved in negative practices, then they will stain you and you will then come and cry for **THE FATHER GOD**. You know that certain types of people are not **GOOD** so why do you go and have something to do with them? Is it because of money, you go and marry a soothsayer or an evil man? Due to someone's position as big man or being rich, you sleep with or marry a negative person. Do you know how such a person managed to get that money? People donate money to **THE FATHER** and do this and that for **GOD** but do **I** want money made from evil practice? If someone puts faeces and urine in the plate for you to eat, will you be as stupid as to eat it or is it because you are blind? Don't you know that **GOD'S** business needs respect? The most disrespectful people are those

The Holy Trinity

who know that they are involved in witchcraft, know that they have evil spirit in them and are practicing evil and are wicked but they still come to the house of **GOD** to donate. On **THE FATHER'S** birthday, you donate. This means that you are the most disrespectful person because you think that **GOD** is blind? You mummer and mock at **GOD**. Just as you murmur with goat, chicken and turkey which you rear and then kill them and eat during the Christmas period. That means that you mock at them.

    Do you think that if that chicken or turkey knew that you intend to kill it, it will eat from your hand again? Do you think that if someone knows that you are a murderer and you will be wicked to him or her that he or she would not desert you? If someone takes you as their friend and loves you but you hate that person, do you think that he or she will love you again when they find out that you hate them? It is because they do not know that you are wicked and so you

The Holy Trinity

hide pretending to be a nice person. Oh peace oh, you will say and **GOD** this and that but you have talisman, you are a member of a secret society, you worship idols and are involved in all sorts of negativisms and are part of negative meetings but when they finish, they would come and preach in the bethel. You are the most disrespectful person to **GOD** and your condemnation would be greater because you are mocking **GOD**. Do you not know that **GOD** means **GOOD** and **GOOD** means a sanitized phenomenon, as something that has nothing to do with evil? Why do you mix things?

Why do you mix darkness and **LIGHT**? You insult the **LIGHT** because to bring darkness to **LIGHT** means that you want to quench the **LIGHT**. And how do you spoil the **LIGHT**? It is to break it out and spoil it because when the **LIGHT** is **GOOD**, you cannot comprehend it. Every wicked man wants to destroy a **GOOD** person because such a person is

The Holy Trinity

LIGHT as someone that speaks the truth and you do not want to see such a person because you think that when that person is around, he or she becomes a threat to you. However, **I** have now put **MY** feet down. Just have faith in **THE FATHER GOD**, sanitize your mind so that **THE FATHER GOD** would live in you, then, let anybody dare to mess about with you and they will see what **I, THE FATHER GOD THE CREATOR OF THE UNIVERSE** will do to them.

Let **MY PEACE** and blessing abide with the entire world now and forevermore, *Amien.*

In the name of Our Lord Jesus the Christ, In the blood of Our Lord Jesus the Christ, Now and forevermore, *Amien.*

THANK YOU FATHER,
THANK YOU FATHER,
THANK YOU FATHER.

Chapter Three

THE INSPIRATIONAL WRITER

**KING SOLOMON SPIRITUAL LIBRARY
THE GOD ENCYCLOPAEDIA
WORD OF INFINITY**

INSPIRATIONAL WRITERS AND READERS OF THE FATHER'S TALK (GOD PRESENT) KING SOLOMON SPIRITUAL LIBRARY

In the name of our Lord Jesus Christ In the blood of our Lord Jesus Christ Now and forever more, Amen

(A) REFERENCING THE FATHER'S TALK (GOD PRESENT) IN KING SOLOMON SPIRITUAL LIBRARY

I know some people will inspire when you visit King Solomon Spiritual Library website or bookshop, and have access to any of **THE FATHER'S TALK (GOD PRESENT)** information through books, electronics, audio and otherwise and are inspired to write or produce any information through the knowledge that you have gained, you must not fail to reference **THE FATHER'S TALK (GOD PRESENT)** in **King Solomon Spiritual Library** as the such of your inspirations.

(B) THE WORD OF TRUTH AND THE HOLY SPIRIT PRINCIPLES

Since **THE FATHER'S TALK (GOD PRESENT)** is the direct information from **THE FATHER GOD ALMIGHTY HIMSELF,** all positive children of God can be, and will be inspired with this **WORD** because the Word of **THE FATHER GOD, THE CREATOR OF THE UNIVERSE** is a Spiritual Case Study for all souls to improve to have self awareness and a Higherself Consciousness.

When you are inspired and you want to write, make sure that your ideas, principles and concepts base on the Holy Spirit of Truth without changing the ordinance of the **FATHER'S TALK (GOD PRESENT).**

(C) THERE SHALL BE CONSEQUENCES THAT WOULD FOLLOW THOSE WHO USE THE MEANING, THE CONCEPTS AND THE PRINCIPLES OF THE FATHER'S TALK (GOD PRESENT) FOR THE PURPOSES OF MISLEADING

Consequences shall follow those who use the meaning, the concepts and the principles of **THE FATHER'S TALK (GOD PRESENT)** for the purposes of misleading in any manner.

Any Human-God, human-animal, human-bird or human-fish who has access to **THE FATHER'S TALK (GOD PRESENT)** through any means, be it via books, electronics, audio and otherwise should know that those words are not the words of human beings. The words are transcribed, proofread and accepted

The Holy Trinity

by **THE FATHER GOD** as it comes from the **SUPREME STUDIO OF THE ALMIGHTY FATHER GOD HIMSELF,** via **King Solomon Spiritual Library.**

When the signal of the information alerts HRM King Solomon David Jesse Etteh from **THE FATHER** through the **COMPREHENSIVE MEMORY OF GOD** in him, at anytime in the day or at night and anywhere, whether on the road or any public place, he will take note of the title of the Revelation Lectures. Sometimes if the location is conducive, lectures can take place immediately. If the location is not conducive, **THE FATHER** fixes the time for the full lecture to take place. Most of the time, some of the lectures take about a week, a month or six months and so on, to deliver when **THE FATHER** brings it back from **HIS SUPREME MEMORY** to HRM King Solomon Etteh.

Take note that the information of **THE FATHER'S TALK (GOD PRESENT)** is not preaching, or the giving of sermons or shared discussion. **THE FATHER** calls it **"*LECTURE REVELATION*"**, which is a Spiritual Case Study for mankind to improve and have the Higherself Consciousness about himself or herself and their creator.

For that reason, every human being that comes across any of this information of the **FATHER'S TALK (GOD PRESENT)** should treat it with utmost and absolute respect and reverence at all times.

HRM King Solomon David Jesse Etteh is not responsible for **THE FATHER'S TALK (GOD PRESENT)** but **GOD HIMSELF. THE ALMIGHTY FATHER** only uses him as a way through, just like a loud speaker from the radio or television receiver.

For this reason, HRM King Solomon David Jesse Etteh will not be held responsible by anyone who does not understand the contents, the concepts and the principles of **THE FATHER'S TALK (GOD PRESENT)** information in King Solomon Spiritual Library. He will not answer any questions or queries from spirit to soul and the physical truth in connection to the above from the lower mind individuals, persons or groups. However, if you are positive and you have love, you are humble, have patience and are peaceful and you want to know and understand more of any part of **THE FATHER'S TALK (GOD PRESENT); 'You should use fasting and prayer'** and or if anyone has any questions in good faith, he or she is free to write to HRM King Solomon and **THE FATHER** in him will respond. He will not, and there is no response to any questions, queries and anything negative with the craftiness of the evil minds of humankind.

That is why you should first read

THE FATHER GOD with **HIS SUPREME HOLY SPIRIT OF TRUTH** will bless all those who read and accept this information with good faith through the name and blood of our Lord Jesus Christ. Amen.

The Holy Trinity

In the name of our Lord Jesus Christ In the blood of our Lord Jesus Christ Now and forever more, Amen

"THEUNISAL-SUREME SEACELION"
The Universal Supreme Season Celebration
=========
"THEUNI-SUREME WORA THECRO-THEUNISE"
The Universal Supreme Word Almighty
The Creator Of The Universe
================
WWW.COME4WORD.COM
THE OFFICIAL SITE FOR
===============
EVERLASTING UNIVERSAL ALL WORD SEASON APPRECIATION CEREMONIAL PROGRAM
==========

THE UNIVERSAL SUPREME ALL WORD SEASON CELEBRATION
(GOD PRESENT)

SOMETHING MORE THAN GOLD IN THE HEART OF ALL MEN IS THE WORD

======================

THE WORD IS THE MAKER, THE SOLE ADMINISTRATOR AND THE CREATOR OF THE UNIVERSE. THEREFORE, ALL MANKIND ON EARTH MUST APPRECIATE THE WORD IN ALL CAPACITIES FOREVER

==============

FROM EVERY OA OF AO TO AO OF AO

The Holy Trinity

**(1ˢᵗ OCTOBER TO 10th OCTOBER.)
YEARLY IS
THE UNIVERSAL SUPREME
ALL WORD SEASON
CELEBRATION TO APPRECIATE
THE FATHER GOD ALMIGHTY
WORDWORDWWORDWORDWORD
WORD
CELEBRATION!
CELEBRATION!!
CELEBRATION!!!
THE
UNIVERSAL
SUPREME WORD
CELEBRATION OF ALL TIME
======
THE ALMIGHTY FATHER GOD,
THE
CREATOR OF ALL THINGS
BROTHERHOOD
ORGANISED BY
KING SOLOMON SPIRITUAL
LIBRARY
======
HRM KING SOLOMON DAVID
JESSE ETE
INSPIRATIONAL HEAD**

The Holy Trinity

IN THE HONOUR OF THE FATHER GOD THE CREATOR OF THE UNIVERSE THE HOLY SPIRIT OF TRUTH AND THE KING OF KINGS AND THE LORD OF LORDS
==========
THANK YOU FATHERo

KING SOLOMON SPIRITUAL LIBRARY THE GOD ENCYCLOPAEDIA WORD OF INFINITY
================
King Solomon Spiritual Library, God Universal Information Centre Father's Talk (God Present)

The Holy Trinity

WITH LOVE

Covered: **This BOOK,** e-book, software or software's, books, website, video, audio, idea or ideas, formula or formulas, manual or instruction manual.

... Hereby gives you a non-exclusive license to use the ... (THIS BOOK). Some of the word here is coded with the (WORD OF SUPER HOLY AND INTELLIGENCE FATHER GOD ALMIGHTY)

Title, ownership rights, and intellectual property rights in and to the Website, Books, E-book, Audios and Videos, Shops and Store – e-Stores, Fundraisings, Celebrations and the supreme word seasons Celebration formulas and arrangement, Positive Inspiration, Holy (Fata), FATHER GOD ALMIGHTY POSSESSING SPIRIT in thought, in words and in did, thinking well, speaking well, hearing well and doing well shall remain in me and in ... The BOOK is protected by international copyright.

FATHER'S TALK (GOD PRESENT)
The message in The Father's Talk (GOD PRESENT) does not challenge any authority either individuals, groups or governments of any land or even any belief of any form. It is rather challenging the truth that is hidden from mankind. Therefore, any spirit, soul or physical human being who decides to challenge this truth shall have himself or herself to blame.

Key A
Any individual that reads any of The Father's Talk (GOD PRESENT) with faith; love and acceptance will experience immediate positive change in his or her life from spirit, soul to physical. If he or she accepts the message then he or she will be free from any evil.

Key B: **PEACE AND LOVE**
If you do not believe the contents of any of The Father's Talk (GOD PRESENT) it is possible through The Father's divine love and peace simply hands over your copy to a friend or somebody else that would like to keep a copy, or signing out from any of the website that connected to The Father's Talk (GOD PRESENT) KING SOLOMON SPIRITUAL e-LIBRARY without any evil and negative comments and you are
blessed and free.
========

FROM THE DESK OF INSPIRATIONAL HEAD
Fees, Prices and Donations; There is no refund on fees, price or donations since your fees price or donations are using as a charity contribution to do administration work of THE SUPREME WORD, So please kindly read this first before you decide to involves yourself in any of the under mention of HRM King Solomon David Jesse ETE universal

Inspirational Businesses of (GOD PRESENT) in cash, kinds and otherwise.

I CAME FROM THE FATHER GOD, WITH THE FATHER GOD, AND BY THE FATHER GOD TO ESTABLISH THE FOLLOWING:

Therefore, all distributors and contributors of The Father's Talk (GOD PRESENT), The Spiritual Advice, Healing and Counselling on General Live (The Universal Supreme Spiritual General Hospital), New Songs and Psalms of King David and Solomon, The Word of **GOD** Processing City in Ikot Okwo or e-City online, The Trinity Celebration, "**OUC FUND**", The Universal Bank Account For All Creations, "**ERUFA**" ETE Royal Universal Family, "**THEUNISAL-SUREME SEACELION**" The Universal Supreme Word Season Celebration To Appreciates THE FATHER GOD ALMIGHTY "**THEUNI-SUREME WORA THECRO-THEUNISE**" The Universal Supreme Word Almighty, **THE CREATOR OF THE UNIVERSE** should

The Holy Trinity

attach this information to all readers, website visitors, distributors, affiliates person/group, celebrant and celebrations centres, supporters and promoters, members, workers and voluntary workers, Ete royal universal palace committee, governments and many other centres as an agreement. Please kindly know that I am not answering to any physical human except **PEACE, UNITY AND LOVE.**

"THEUNISAL-SUREME WORA THECRO-THEUNISE".

I AM IN THE STAGE OF SUPER HOLY AND INTELLIGENCE FATHER GOD POSITIVE MADNESS OF THE HOLY SPIRIT OF TRUTH,
ENYEN ODUDU ODUDU ODUDU ABASI MI OOO ZIM ZIM ZIM ASSASU, POSITIVE POSITIVE POSITIVE.
UKEMEKE AKA IDIOK UNAM.
Let the peace and blessing of the Holy Father abide with everybody who corporate with this divine Father's Talk (GOD PRESENT

THANK YOU FATHER

BY
THE HOLY SPIRIT OF
THE FATHER GOD
THROUGH HIS SERVANT
Senior Christ Servant
HRM King Solomon David Jesse ETE
Brotherhood of the
Cross and STAR
Eteroyal Universal family
Ikot Okwo The Great City of Refuge,
Ete Community
Ikot Abasi LGA-543001
Akwa Ibom State Nigeria-W/A
Tel. 08036693841
www.ksslibrary.com
Email: ksslibrary@eteroyalmail.com

The Holy Trinity

READ AT LEAST SEVEN LECTURE'S REVELATIONS BEFORE YOU CAN MAKE ANY COMMENTS

In the Name of Our Lord Jesus Christ In the Blood of Our Lord Jesus Christ
Now and forever more

Everybody should have access and read at least seven **FATHER'S TALK (GOD PRESENT)** Lecture's Revelations before you can make any comments about it. If you do not go through at least seven **FATHER'S TALK** lectures and you comment you may make mistakes. When you make mistakes your blood will be upon you because you would have taken voluntary evolution to misquote **THE FATHER GOD THE CREATOR OF THE UNIVERSE.** If however, you go through any seven of **THE FATHER'S TALK (GOD PRESENT)** –
one of **THE FATHER'S TALK** stands for one Spirit of God, which means that **FATHER'S TALK GOD PRESENT**

The Holy Trinity

Lectures Revelation are witness by the Seven Spirits of God, which **I** use as the Seven Church of God and Seven days of the Week, Seven spirits of Creations in one Supreme energy of THE FATHER GOD, THE SPOKEN WORD.

When you read seven **FATHER'S TALK L**ectures then, **I THE FATHER GOD** will reveal you as positive person. Then you will have a portion in **ME**. One of **THE FATHER'S TALK** will have a portion in you. Then you would know that this information came from **THE FATHER GOD.**

The Father's Talk God Present is not a mere talk from a man!

In the Name of Our Lord Jesus Christ In the Blood of Our Lord Jesus Christ
Now and forever more
WWW.THEWORDCITY.COM
www.ksslibrary.com

THE UNIVERSAL SUPREME ACKNOWLEDGEMENT

'THE ONLY SOURCE AND REMEDY TO END ALL HUMANITIES PROBLEMS'

Join me to Celebrate; Acknowledge, Appreciates and give full RECOGNITION to
THE UNIVERSAL SUPREME WORD,
YOUR LIFE FORCE,
THE TOTALITY OF ALL TOTALITIES
YOUR CREATOR,
THE FATHER GOD ALMIGHTY,
THE CREATOR OF THE UNIVERSE

WWW.COME4WORD.COM
Contact EMAIL:
hrmkingsolomon@eteroyalmail.com

THANK YOU FATHER

ESTABLISH MY SPIRITUAL LIBRARY

I THE FATHER GOD ALMIGHTY THE SUPREME WORD OF THE UNIVERSE AM THE SPIRITUAL FOOD TO FEED YOUR SOUL. Therefore, **I** want every family in this world, every home in this world, every office, government offices, monarchies, countries, states, regions, counties, communities, local authorities compound, family homes, everyone everywhere should be collecting published copies of **THE EVERLASTING GOSPEL AND THE FATHER'S TALK (GOD PRESENT)** Lectures Revelations of KING SOLOMON SPIRITUAL LIBRARY should be established physically in your houses. So that everybody should have those RECORDS. Go to read the books regularly. Every family should have this Library **MY** INFORMATION CENTRE for their family members.

Every generation of the particular family could easily go to their family Library of KING SOLOMON SPIRITUAL LIBRARY EVERLASTING GOSPEL and the **FATHER'S TALK (GOD PRESENT) Lectures Revelations** and read the Gospels and Lectures Revelations. Generations upon generations will access their KING SOLOMON SPIRITUAL LIBRARY.

You must all have **THE LIBRARY OF THE FATHER GOD ALMIGHTY** called **KING SOLOMON SPIRITUAL LIBRARY FATHER'S TALK (GOD PRESENT) LECTURES REVELATIONS** in your homes and offices. The authorities and individuals concerned must see to that. When you establish your branch of KING SOLOMON SPIRITUAL LIBRARY and have Everlasting Gospels and the **FATHER'S TALK (GOD PRESENT)** Lectures Revelations that place is blessed and secured. In the name and Blood of Our Lord Jesus Christ, now and forever more, Amen.

THANK YOU FATHER

The Holy Trinity

The Holy Trinity

The title List of some of the **Father's Talk (GOD Present)**

1: THE MANUAL OF THE SPOKEN WORD

2: THE MANUAL OF LIFE

3: INVESTMENT WITH GOD

4: ISO IBOT EDEM IBOT

5: THE CHARACTER OF THE NEW WORLD

6: HELPMANTRANS

7: UNDERSTANDING MY WORD

8: TRUTH, POSITION, POST AND NAME

9: NON STOP BLESSING

10: IMPRESSION

11: STAGES OF EDUCATIONS (SPE, SSE & SUE)

12: THE ENGINEERING OF LIFE
13: THE CONTENT PACKAGE

14: THE BUDGET OF THE NEW WORLD

15: DIVINE ATTENTION

16: THE BABY SPIRIT

17: PROMOTION

18: ADVANCE AND PROGRESSING MIND

19: THE TEMPLE OF THE LIVING GOD

20: I AM OK

21: THE SPIRIT OF TRUTH

22: THE PERFECT PERMANENCY

23: THE FATHER GOD, GOD, GOD THE FATHER

24: HUSBAND, WIFE AND CHILD

25: GOD AND HIS HARBINGER

26: LIFE EVERLASTING

27: POSSESS

28: MY MIND AND MY PLAN

29: AFTER HEART AND AFTER MIND

30: MY DECLARATION & STAND IN BCS

31: BEYOND THE HOPE OF FAITH

32: MENTAL STAIN

33: THE PRINCIPLE OF SELF HOLD

34: THE MASTERSHIP

35: HIDU-CUM

36: THE UNIVERSAL PARENT

37: ADVANCED YOU AND ME

38: THE GREAT UNIVERSAL CHANGE

39: THE PROJECTED MIND

40: INDESTRUCTIBLE BLESSED FIVE STARS

41: ASTROTS, GOD PRESENT I AND MY FATHER

42: SONGS THE COMPLETION

43: THE RIGHT BUTTON

44: AKWA ABASI IBOM- ETE - DIRECTING NDITO AKWA IBOM

45: THE DIGITAL AGE

46: GOD IS OFFICIAL CHAMPION

47: A TRUE WITNESS

48: MYSTERY OF PROCREATION AND BIRTH

49: THE UNIVERSAL UMBRELLA

50: THE FORERUNNER

51: A OF A TO Z (FIRST OF ALL)

52: MAN IN THREE CAPACITIES

53: THE TRUE LIFE OF HOLY SPIRIT PERSONIFIED

54: IN-BETWEEN THE FATHER & THE SON

55: DIVINE ARRANGEMENT & AUTHORITY

56: TWENTY FIRST CENTURY IS NOT FOR SATAN

57: THE SUPREME WORD SEASON CELEBRATION

58: THE MAXIMUM DEITY

59: TRANSFORMER TRANSMITTER AND WAVE

60: THE SUPREME FUTURE

61: THE BYLOVE OF WORD

62: THE SIGNATURE OF THE FATHER GOD

63: THE TWO WAYS

64: THE UNDERSTANDING OF LIFE

65: THE GREATER THAN SOLOMON IS HERE

66: THE CONQUEROR

67: THE SPIRITUAL GENERAL INSPECTOR OF LIFE

68: THE NIGERIA IN THE AFRICA Part one

69: THE NIGERIA IN THE AFRICA Part two

70: THE CREATOR AND CREATIONS PART ONE

71: THE CREATOR AND CREATIONS PART TWO

72: THE CREATOR AND CREATIONS PART THREE

73: THE SUPREME TEACHER

74: THE SPIRITUAL COVER

75: THE NIGERIA IN THE AFRICA PART THREE

76: THE SUPREME BELIEVE

77: CAST AND BAN (LECTURE IN LIVERPOOL)

78: LIFE EXTENSION MANUAL

79: THE SPIRITUAL TRAFFIC

80: THE VOICE OF THE CREATOR

81: MY OFFICE

82: LIFE SPIRITUAL FIRE EXTINGUISHER

83: INFORMATION

84: FATHER GOD FINAL ARRANGEMENT

85: THE LOVERS OF CHRIST

86: I LOVE YOU, I LOVE YOU TOO

87: THE UNIVERSAL SUPREME UPDATE

88: THE SUPREME ALTAR

89: THE SOURCE AND DESTINATION

90: A SON LIKE THE FATHER THE KING OF KINGS A ROOTS FROM HEAVEN (NOT THIS TIME AROUND)

91: THE TRUE WITNESS AND THE TRUE SERVANT

92: THE FINAL ARRANGEMENT

93: A TRUE NIGERIAN MAN AND WOMAN

94: EVERYONE MUST PERSONALLY INVOLVE

95: BEWARE

96: ESIEN EMANA AKPAN "THE AFRICAN PROBLEMS"

97: THE SECRET OF THE UNIVERSAL PROBLEMS AND THE REMEDY (MUSLIM AND CHRISTIAN FROM THE SAME PARENT)

98: MMU-UDIM – THE BLESSED MOTHER (ABASI ME UDIM)

99: THINK WELL, SPEAK WELL AND DO WELL

100: THE STAGES OF HOW TO PROCESS THE WORD

101: EVIL STAIN, WHO RUNS AWAY FROM WHO

102: BEYOND HUMAN KNOW PURELY SPIRITUAL

103: <u>THE INSPIRATIONAL WRITER</u>

104: BIAKPAN OBIO AKPAN ABASI (THE NEW JERUSALEM CITY)

105: "OBAMA" THE STRAINTHEN AND THE SPIRIT OF BILL GATE AND MICROSOFT

106: **THE HOLY TRINITY**

107: AMEN –ODUWEM IKO ABASI THANK YOU FATHER

www.ingramcontent.com/pod-product-compliance
Lightning Source LLC
Chambersburg PA
CBHW021847300426
44115CB00005B/49